LITTLE BOOK OF
SCOOTERS

LITTLE BOOK OF
SCOOTERS

First published in the UK in 2012

© G2 Entertainment Limited 2013

www.G2ent.co.uk

Printed and bound in China

ISBN 978-1-907803-45-1

Contents

4   Introduction

12   A Stuttering Start

16   From Standing Room Only

32   Taking to the Air – Scooters in Combat

40   Back on Civvy Street

48   Italian Chic – Enter Two Legends

66   Imitation is the Sincerest Form of Flattery!

74   French Fancies and British Eccentricity

84   Jules Verne Would Have Been Proud

96   A Racing Pedigree

104 A New Era

112 The Threes

124 A Cult Following

134 Lost in Translation

Introduction

A 'scooter' is usually described as a two-wheeled motorcycle sometimes fitted with a sidecar but consisting of small wheels, step-through bodywork that encloses the major mechanical components, and a platform for the operator's feet or two foot-rests. There are many variations on the concept that still come under the category but when the idea was first mooted, the aim was to build a light two-wheeled vehicle that was easier to ride and maintain than a motorcycle, whilst providing better level of protection for the rider's clothing. Body panelling will at the very least enclose the engine but can include a front fairing, leg shields and built-in storage boxes. A major difference between a motorcycle and a scooter is that the motorcycle's engine is fixed within the frame whereas, in many cases, the motor on a scooter is either attached directly to the rear axle or swings independently to the main chassis.

The origins of the scooter can be traced as far back as the late-19th Century when vehicle invention and experimentation was still in its infancy. Yet it was not until the late 1950s that the scooter as we would recognise it today had become an established, reliable and easy to manage means of personal transport.

In the pioneering years around the turn of the 20th Century, many manufacturers were marketing motorised vehicles amounting to little more than pedal cycles powered by small and neat

Above: *Vespas and Lambrettas gather at the 2011 Organford Scooter Rally.*

clip-on engines. As a cheaper alternative to the motorcycle, this idea was gradually developed into the lightweight moped and subsequently the mini-bike, a type that would play a significant role during the dark days of World War II. Robust construction and with folding or collapsible capabilities, these machines saw service in various theatres of war and were especially favoured by air divisions. Easily packed into the hold of an aircraft or parachuted within a canister onto the battlefield, mini-bikes were used by troops who were trained to quickly assemble and operate them to aid a rapid advance towards the enemy lines.

After the war, European firms that had been engaged in the supply of armaments sought other ways to exploit their manufacturing capacity and smart and luxurious scooters were launched featuring colourful and stylish 'bodywork' – a welcome relief after the preceding six years of austerity. These

machines were characterised by their step-through access and, with practice, the relative ease with which they could be ridden. Handling the larger diameter wheel moped was not too dissimilar to riding a bicycle whereas the balance and operation of a scooter initially took a little more getting used to.

Scooters, however, attracted a huge number of women customers proving to be more manageable than the heavy and somewhat cumbersome motorcycle. The 'body' panelling meant clothing remained free from engine grime, road dust, and mud, and with the option of a full-length fairing, a rider could be relatively well-protected from inclement weather.

With a boom in post-war sales, two Italian firms emerged as industry leaders

LITTLE BOOK OF **SCOOTERS**

and while Innocenti's Lambretta and Piaggio's Vespa became the benchmark of chic design, many other famous manufacturers tapped into the market at one time or another. As the popularity of scootering spread, clubs were soon formed, meeting at weekends or at specially organised rallies across the country. One of the first to do so was the Manchester Lambretta Club (later The Lyons) which held its first get-together over a greengrocers shop in 1954.

Among youths of the 'modern community', the scooter became very much the fashion accessory especially during the mid-1960s. Bitter rivalry, however, led to notorious bank holiday clashes between the scooter-loving

'Mods' and the old guard of Rockers who still preferred the classic British single-cylinder bikes and café racers. In reality, these scuffles were few and far between but the tabloid newspapers chose to brand all scooter-riding Mods as troublemakers, stirring up public hostility against many who had simply chosen to adopt a new fashion or purchase a cheap form of transport.

Nevertheless, for Mods, a completely separate lifestyle began to evolve with devotees choosing to dress in a unique style of clothing designed by a fresh breed and avant-garde generation of fashion houses. Many scooter owners further stamped their individuality by customising machines with artwork or by attaching items from the enormous range of accessories on offer.

In recent times there has been a resurgence of interest in scootering, fuelled by celebrating those first post-war Italian machines that originally set the standard, and that others could only hope to emulate. In the last twenty years, numerous manufacturers have responded by unveiling modern or retro-styled models to meet the demand of a new generation of enthusiasts.

In the sixteen years I worked at The National Motor Museum Trust, Beaulieu, I could always find time to have a good look round some of the fantastic machines that made up the motorcycle collection. Tucked away and almost overlooked in their separate section of the building, famous marques such as AJS, Douglas, Norton and Vincent were interspersed with a sprinkling of iconic scooters from the post-war boom years including examples of the BSA Sunbeam, Dürkopp Diana, Innocenti Lambretta and Piaggio Vespa. In addition there were one or two exhibits representative of the early experimental period of the 1920s such as the ABC Skootamota, Autoglider, Mobile Pup and Ner-a-car. It is only natural that scooters will never be everybody's cup of tea but it was always fascinating to see how inventive some of these firms had become in their attempts to get 'The Masses' mobile with a cheap-to-buy and economic form of two-wheeled transport.

In putting this book together, I would like to thank the following individuals for their help with technical and historical information, and for the use of some fine scooter images:

Simon Balistrari; Clive Bassett of the Harrington Covert Museum, Northamptonshire; Patrick Collins of the Reference Library, Jon Day of the Motoring Picture Library, and Doug Hill, Mike Moore, Derek Ward and Andrew Wise at The National Motor Museum, Beaulieu; Mary Brisson at the Petersen Automotive Museum, Los Angeles; Roy Butler; Helen Ford; Jules Gammond; Anna Giordano of New Rochelle, New York; Dale Johnson at The Tank Museum, Bovington; Christof Kipfer of Switzerland who manages a website dedicated to the products of Velosolex (www.velo-solex.ch); Matthew Lombard of the Australian National Motor Museum, Birdwood; Andrew Mulcahy at the Ariel 3 Museum, Brislington; James Peacop at the Mouldsworth Motor Museum, Cheshire; Archie Pearce; Danny Rees; Johan Schaeverbeke at the Oldtimer Motoren Museum, Belgium; James Starrett; Ian Williamson for the very kind loan of his camera; and members of the various scooter clubs up and down the country who without fail have been more than happy to offer advice and impart details about their own beautifully restored machines. Last but by no means least, I would like to show my wholehearted appreciation to my Dad, Mike Lanham, whose enthusiasm for all things transport-orientated and willingness to help out in any way he can has always proved invaluable with the projects I have undertaken. Thank you all.

Steve Lanham
2012

A Stuttering Start

It was more than 140 years ago that the first pioneering inventors attempted to harness any form of self-propelled motive power aboard a two wheeled carriage. During the mid-1800s, steam engines were the 'latest thing' but proved too heavy and cumbersome for the comparatively spindly cycle frames of the day. In an era when it was rare to find a road with a decent flat surface, these experimental machines were naturally unstable and dangerous to ride. Aside from the fact that other road-borne vehicles consisted almost entirely of carriages and waggons pulled by livestock including the horse, an animal that could easily be alarmed in the presence of a 'living' hissing steam engine, these early contraptions required constant attention in order to keep a good fire burning and the right level of water in the boiler. It was not until the introduction of the internal combustion engine that a more successful motorcycle-type vehicle could finally be made.

At a time when the first rickety motor spirit-powered autocars were taking to the road, Rinaldo Piaggio was establishing a foundry and railway works in Genoa, Italy, to build steam locomotives and carriages, more than sixty years before his son, Enrico, would embark on the construction of a form of transport that sparked an enormous wave of enthusiasm.

In the meantime, the greatest steps towards scooter mass production took place in France and Germany towards the end of the 1800s. By then, compact petrol motors were being assembled in large numbers and sold to engineering firms previously known for their pedal cycle manufacture, who in turn were then constructing 'bicyclettes'. These were in essence existing bicycles transformed into self-propelled machines with the addition of a clip-on engine attachment. Many businesses that later became household names and major players within the motor industry such as Raleigh, Matchless, Ariel and Rover began trading in this way but it was in 1894

that the German engineers Heinrich and Wilhelm Hildebrand teamed up with Alois Wolfmüller to construct a machine that would subsequently be considered as the real forerunner to the scooter. The 'Motorrad' had a purpose-built low step-through frame of dual parallel tubing that cradled an enormous 1,489cc four-stroke petrol engine fed by a combined fuel tank and vaporizer. The hollow rear mudguard doubled as a primitive radiator with the water contained within it flowing through a jacket surrounding the horizontal twin-cylinders and cooling them. Two pistons providing direct drive to the rear wheel via a pair of connecting rods and a lack of pedals or any form of

clutch meant that the machine required push starting. Once on the move, however, the Motorrad could achieve a commendable 28 miles per hour. Out of several hundred completed bikes, only five examples are known to exist today – all on public display in Museums around the world.

But it was not until the turn of the 20th Century when something remotely resembling what today would be described as a scooter first appeared. Built in Blois in the Loir-et-Cher Department of Central France, the Auto-Fauteuil was a machine consisting of a much lower step-through frame and smaller wheels

than the contemporary motorcycles. Although it lacked any form of body panelling, the Auto-Fauteuil did feature foot-boards on either side of a centrally mounted battery box and a wrap-around seat rest. Its low road stance therefore offered its owner the kind of comfortable riding position more associated with a scooter than a motorcycle.

In the years leading up to World War I, there were many ideas put forward for small two-wheelers. Very few of these, however, were fortunate enough to make it past the drawing board stage and even then rarely progressed beyond a prototype machine.

Above: *Rather than attach a separate motor to an existing bicycle frame, Perks and Birch of Coventry offered a replacement rear wheel containing an engine within the rim.*

From Standing Room Only

In the modern era there has been a growing fad among teenagers to own a type of high-speed machine that instead of a saddle, only has a foot-board yet possesses a diminutive but comparatively powerful engine that gives high-speed performance. Unfortunately, their use has often lead to a spate of unsociable behaviour in residential areas with ignorant and largely inexperienced riders taking to footpaths and pavements, repeatedly causing alarm to pedestrians, and proving the bane of traffic cops. Although this craze is something of a recent phenomenon, a no-frills motorised two-wheeler, where operating one is performed standing on a flat platform with all controls located on the handlebars, is by no means a new concept.

The idea of the stand-up scooter can trace its origins right back to just before World War I. In Long Island City, New York, the Auto-Ped was in essence a development of the child's ride-on scooter toy. In front of the trailing wheel it had a platform on which its owner would stand and a set of what would initially appear to be unsophisticated handlebars. These could be folded flat against the platform when not in use, so that the Auto-Ped required only a small amount of space when being stored. On the handlebars were lights, horn, lubrication and throttle controls, the latter being connected via a cable

FROM STANDING ROOM ONLY

Above: *In 1920, Felix Hudlass made a prototype stand-on scooter at his Southport Works in Lancashire. It was probably the only two-wheeler he made and was better known for his three and four-wheeler cars.*

Centre: *1921 DKW Golem.*

to the motor. This was a 155cc 1.5hp four-stroke unit located directly over the front wheel below the headstock and so steered as one with the wheel. Operating the machine worked off a combined clutch/brake system whereby moving the handlebars forward, the clutch would engage through a series of friction plates and gears, with speed being determined by the throttle. By pulling the handlebars back, the clutch would disengage whilst simultaneously applying the brakes. In July 1913, a patent was applied for and eventually granted in 1916, a year after

full production had already commenced. In the intervening period, the fuel reservoir had been redesigned so that it was now a conventional tank above the engine – on pre-production promotional material, it had been suggested that the void within the hollow steering column would be utilised for this purpose. Instead the handlebar tube now contained the engine lubricating oil.

With a top speed of only 20 miles per hour but with reasonable fuel consumption in a time of shortages, the Auto-Ped proved popular particularly

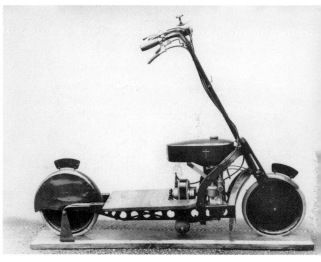

amongst well-to-do New Yorkers and went on general sale in 1915. It soon fell out of favour after the war, however, when better equipped vehicles such as light cars and cyclecars became more readily available. Production in America ceased in 1921 whilst in Europe the model lasted one further year as the Krupp-Roller.

Krupp was one of Germany's oldest manufacturing firms and was originally founded in the Ruhr Valley as far back as the 1500s. Throughout World War I, workers conscripted from occupied

Belgium were brought overland to Essen and were employed in fabricating ammunition for the armed forces and built over eighty U-boats as well as a cargo-carrying submarine. With the peace declaration of 1918, the Allied nations imposed strict reparations on the German Empire and the other countries making up the Central Powers (the Austro-Hungarian Empire, the Ottoman Empire and the Kingdom of Bulgaria) which included a ban on the manufacture of armaments. Krupp looked into other areas of engineering and, alongside its

Above: *The 1½hp shaft-driven Alwin of 1920 ran on solid tyres.*

Above: The
142cc Kenilworth
represented
one of the more
comfortable
scooters of the
1920s. This
example is owned
by American
collector, Jerry
Perkins.

main output of heavy machinery and steam railway locomotives, a flow line was designated for making scooters. Built between 1919 and 1922, the Krupp-Roller was almost identical to the Auto-Ped but featured a slightly more powerful 191cc 1.7hp engine of the German company's own design.

It was around the same period that the stand-up scooter was finding a small number of enthusiasts in Britain. Sir Henry Norman and Major A. M. Low tried to promote a slightly improved version of the Auto-Ped but their Norlow fell at the first hurdle when they were unable to secure enough financial

Left: *The Stafford Auto-Scooters Mobile-Pup was initially designed as a stand-on machine but gained a seat in 1921.*

backing. Nevertheless, the London firm, Kingsbury – formerly known for their aircraft engines – became one of the main advocates of the concept. Their offering had an improved layout with the 150cc 2hp two-stroke unit removed from the front wheel and placed in a more conventional position within the main frame. Locating the engine behind the headstock provided slightly better stability and considerably shifted the centre of

gravity. Although it was advertised as economical transport "…for honest hard work…" and "…ideal for shopping expeditions…", a lack of carrying space other than the rider's platform meant the Kingsbury Scooter was probably only suited to one of its other claimed benefits as a "…mount for a country spin…"!

An almost identical machine was marketed by the Alwin Manufacturing Company, Teddington but where the

Kingsbury was chain driven, the Alwin featured shaft transmission as well as a pressed steel sprung frame.

With the signing of the Armistice in 1918 came a spate of activity amongst the industrialised nations to get the general population out and about again – an attempt to return to the kind of peacetime normality enjoyed before 1914. The automobile engineering community, especially in Europe, was putting a great deal of effort into the development of small affordable cars with an eye firmly focussed on the family market. Other businesses that in the past had traditionally built motorcycles, bicycles or even small scale light machinery looked to scooters and mopeds as a way of providing adults, especially the younger generations, with a solution to an apparent lack of cheap motorised transport. The easiest solution that in preceding years had provided adequate results was to attach a proprietary engine to a simple bicycle frame. There were a number of firms who could supply these small and compact units off the shelf and the British built-Autosco was a typical example of this approach. Made in London by Brown and Layfield, the Autosco was almost identical to a contemporary design unveiled by the Briggs-Stratton Company of Milwaukee, comprising of an open bicycle-type frame, a 117cc motor attached directly to the rear wheel, and a fuel tank sited above the rear mudguard. Marseel were another firm tapping into this market although their 232cc model at least had its single-cylinder engine concealed horizontally under the foot-board driving the rear wheel via a chain.

But other inventors were prepared to start from scratch and only an ill-conceived design or poor business acumen would see them fail.

In the German town of Zwickau, two Danish engineers called Rasmussen and Mathiessen had initially built an experimental steam car and named it Dampf Kraft Wagen or DKW for short, but in 1919 Rasmussen began construction of a prototype motorcycle which he later christened Das Kleiner Wunder (The Little Wonder). The following year, the DKW Golem would represent Rasmussen's first foray into the light two-wheeler market. This was quickly followed by the another model, the Lomos of 1922, which was a step-through open-framed scooter with relatively small wheels, a seat with wrap-round back rest, and a mesh guard

Far Left: *The Autoglider was one of the quirkier scooters of the early-1920s.*

to protect the rider's legs from the 118cc engine's flywheel. An interesting feature was that the hollow seat rest also doubled as the fuel tank! So successful was Rasmussen's early designs that within a decade, DKW had become the largest motorcycle manufacturer in the world.

Back in Britain and taking inspiration from Kingsbury's efforts of 1919, Captain George Thomas Smith-Clarke decided to build something similar for his wife as a runabout in around their home town of Kenilworth. This had comparatively larger wheels than the Kingsbury and a French-made Clement motor fitted in an off-set position on the frame. It certainly caught the attention of cycle agents Booth Brothers of Coventry who, with their own addition of a sprung seat and superior Norman 142cc unit, re-branded it under the Kenilworth Utility Motors badge. Owners of a Kenilworth also had the luxury of electric lighting – not that riding such a machine at the dead of night was particularly advisable!

Across the city, the Mobile-Pup was unveiled by Stafford Auto-Scooters Ltd, part of a sizeable organisation called T.G. John Ltd which would later evolve into the famous car manufacturer,

Alvis. Priced new at £47, the Pup was one of the more expensive models on the market as well as being one of the ugliest! Consisting of an open frame and large diameter wheels, its cylindrical fuel tank perched precariously forward of the headstock, the 142cc single-cylinder motor was mounted at an angle in-line with the front forks, and the exhaust pipe hung limp like a dead snake to one side of the front wheel! From the results, it is hard to believe that a great deal of serious planning could have gone into this ramshackle contraption. Nevertheless, for a year or so, considerable orders for the Pup were received despite only minor changes being made to the overall layout.

Only a few miles away, the staff of Autoglider Limited set about honing their rather attractive 2½hp model in Great Charles Street, Birmingham. Initially this was also of stand-up design but like the Auto-Ped had its 270cc Villiers engine mounted over the front wheel. In trials, a brace of Autogliders were ridden non-stop for over 100 miles, an exercise not uncommon in the days before state-of-the-art computerised technology, and the only way of testing whether essential improvements or adjustments were needed before a final public unveiling.

In order to appeal to a wider customer base, a plywood box displaying some rather stylish curves was added over the Autoglider's rear wheel topped with a padded full-width seat. By 1920, six variations had been prepared for that year's Olympia Show including one for rider and pillion passenger and a sporting version aimed at the hell-raiser who could wind this rather delicate-looking creature up to a terrifying 50 miles per hour! The management were confident of good sales and in their advertisement advised that any show-goer searching for them should "Look for the most crowded Stand…"! Interest compared to its competitors was promising but by the mid-1920s, both Autoglider and their local rivals, Kenilworth, had been consigned to history.

Not so successful was the dreary-looking Macklum, born out of the imagination of F. MacCallum and built in the Birmingham works of Alfred Wiseman & Co., Ltd. It was very similar to the Autoglider with small diameter wheels and utilised the same 292cc proprietary engine positioned directly over the front wheel. The only major difference was that it was fitted with a seat that represented nothing more than

a thin flat pad mounted on six springs on top of a square box containing the battery. The Macklum was not pretty and riding one could not have been a comfortable experience.

Likewise, the ill-conceived Silva, made in London by T. and T. Motors Ltd would struggle in a beauty contest! With its 117cc motor attached to one side of the large front wheel and a puny rear wheel of less than half the diameter trailing behind the wide footboard, it would be understandable if any rider, even during an era of such experimentation, was subjected to a tirade of ridicule from any kid fortunate enough to see one in action!

Another concern was the All British Engine Company Ltd established by Ronald Charteris in 1911. A year after business commenced, Charteris began selling to other manufacturing firms an in-house designed petrol motor conceived from the creative mind of talented Chief Engineer, Granville Bradshaw. It was Bradshaw who pioneered and patented the transverse flat-twin long before BMW had adopted it for their own two-wheelers during the 1920s, and when they did, Bradshaw contested the move and took the Bavarian company to court.

After the war, Charteris's company changed its name to ABC Motors Ltd and embarked on promoting the Skootamota, a 123cc machine comprising

Above: *1922 Reynolds Runabout.*

of rudimentary low-slung frame, wide foot-board and simple bicycle-type handlebars and stem. ABC chose to locate the engine behind the rider and over the rear wheel with transmission provided via a short chain so that it was completely unobtrusive to the operator. Dismissing the standing idea, ABC furnished the machine with a saddle enhancing rider comfort and stability and with this layout the Skootamota proved to be a relative success finding buyers right across Europe.

In the years immediately following World War I, the likes of Monet & Goyon, Ner-a-car, Reynolds and Unibus took the seated riding position one or two steps closer to luxury. The machines of Monet & Goyon and Reynolds, for example, were fully sprung and provided backrest support on all their models. Monet & Goyon's 'Vélauto' displayed a quite splendid interwoven cane basket seat whilst Reynolds tried to capture the attention of the sporting gentleman and his lady friend by fitting to its Runabout a swivelling pillion seat so that the female passenger, if so desired, could ride side-saddle!

The term 'Uni bus' might today throw up visions of acne-ridden students in some worn out 15-seater Ford Transit (well that's how it was for the author anyway), but in post-war Cheltenham it was quite a different story. Between 1920 and 1922, the Gloster Aircraft Company constructed

Right: *A superb period shot of the Ner-a-car which was built in Britain from 1921 to 1927.*

the Unibus – a scooter whose remarkable looks, bearing a striking resemblance to some of the styling exercises emerging some thirty or so years later, would ultimately spell its downfall. To shroud the channel-section frame, designer Harold Boultbee used pressed aluminium panels and sculpted a beautifully smooth two-piece body with hardly a straight line apart from the flat foot-board. The front section that comprised of the leg shields and mudguard housed the 269cc Villiers engine and two-speed gearbox. At the rear, the rider's seat acted as a lid to a handy storage compartment – a feature almost universally incorporated

in today's machines. The company tried to win orders by publicising it as "…the car on two wheels…" but the Unibus's revolutionary looks were too radical for the time. Slow sales were further compounded by a price tag of almost £100 with few possessing the means to afford one.

Equally advanced for its time was the Ner-a-car although in terms of size and weight was more akin to a motorcycle than its contemporary scooters. The name 'Ner-a-car' might sound as if it was again trying to emulate Gloster Aircraft Company's claim that the Unibus was

"…the car on two wheels…", but by some happy coincidence it was in fact a play on its creators name, American inventor Carl Neracher. Even though the first examples were assembled Stateside, British car maker Sheffield-Simplex announced at the 1921 Isle of Man TT that it would commence production at both its Tinsley and Finningley works. The first home-grown Ner-a-car differed only slightly from its American counterpart in that the clever monocoque bodywork which acted as a stressed member housed a Sheffield-Simplex 211cc two-stroke unit powering a crankshaft laid longitudinally within the frame. The transmission was a rather fussy and not entirely reliable affair. At the end of the crankshaft was a flywheel which was in direct contact with a secondary friction wheel that rotated a final chain drive to the rear road wheel. Equally unusual was the use of pushrod linkage between handlebars and the front wheel.

In 1923, all manufacture of Ner-a-cars was transferred to Kingston-upon-Thames and a new model, the 'B', was announced. This was a more powerful bike benefiting from a 285cc engine but when in only a year or so the 'C' was introduced with its 350cc Blackburne motor, the unorthodox and out-dated friction/chain transmission was replaced by a more conventional gearbox unit. The Ner-a-car was one of the success stories of the 1920s. Women seemed to be especially enamoured with its low-slung step-through bodywork and rakish lines, and according to listings published by the Society of Motor Manufacturers and Traders (SMMT), it lasted almost into the following decade. As many as 6,500 examples left the factory before production ended in the late-1920s.

Throughout the twenty or so years that separated the two World Wars, a

race developed between British motor manufacturers, especially Austin, Ford and Morris to build a small car that could adequately convey a typical size family. The ultimate goal was to be the first company to profit from the '£100 car', but over time the likes of Austin's Seven, Morris's Minor and Ford's Model Y were joined by numerous light cars and

cyclecars. With many small backstreet businesses starting up and trying their hand at vehicle production, British city high streets soon became crowded with a fascinating and eclectic mix of transportation. The likes of Carden, J.M.B., Singer and Trojan, all marques long forgotten today, jockeyed for a slice of the market and by the 1930s, those wishing to acquire a cheap-to-buy and economical form of low-powered car could choose from a huge range of vehicles on offer. Unfortunately, the amount of affordable competition heralded a decline in scooter production and certainly on European soil it would not be until the 1950s that the concept became significantly popular again.

Taking to the Air - Scooters in Combat

For the British armed services, mechanised transport came into its own during the Boer War when traction engines were put to use hauling troop and ammunition wagons as well as the heaviest guns across wild and largely unpaved terrain. By World War I, many governments around the globe had instigated a program of building a range of different vehicles that could aid their armed forces in times of conflict. Two-wheelers found their place among the ranks with bicycles forming a convenient means of mobility that might once have been the domain of the horse. During World War II, the motorcycle proved indispensable for rapidly dispatching orders and messages between points of contact and, especially when fitted with a sidecar, was particularly effective for carrying machine gun equipment or as an escort vehicle for convoys of heavy transport.

The diminutive proportions of the scooter did not go unnoticed either. Lt. Colonel John R.V. Dolphin was Commanding Officer at the Special Operations Executive (SOE) Station IX, the Inter-Services Research Bureau near Welwyn Garden City. He realised that the scooter was a form of transport that could possibly benefit the vital work his recruits were training to carry out. The role of the SOE Agent was to join forces with the local Resistance groups in various parts of German occupied Europe and cause

Left: *A Welbike being loaded aboard a Douglas C47 in 1944.*

sabotage and subversion against the enemy forces. In the early years of the war, Dolphin assigned avid motorcycle rider, Harry Lester, the task of designing a lightweight machine that could be conveniently stowed in the hold of an aircraft fuselage or more importantly collapsed to fit into an airdrop canister. These standard-size cylindrical containers were made in their thousands for parachuting behind enemy lines, and could accommodate all manner of equipment crucial to the advancing Allies including supplies of ammunition, food, protective clothing and helmets. The vehicle, therefore, had to conform to the restrictions of the canister, the dimensions being 4 foot 3 inches x 15 inches x 12 inches.

Lester's endeavours eventually produced a 98cc prototype, a machine devoid of all unessential features that, through the absence of suspension, front brakes or any form of lights, further pushed the boundaries of rudimentary. In transit, the handlebars and foot-rests were folded flat to the frame and the saddle lowered into the stem tube. A series of proving tests were performed with the prototype before the War Office gave the go ahead for a batch of Villiers Spryt-engined examples to be made by the Excelsior Motor Company of Birmingham. These were then sent for further evaluation at RAF Sherburn in Yorkshire before full production of the 'Welbike', as it would eventually be called, could commence.

In total nearly 4,000 units were dispatched in various theatres of the war, most falling into the hands of the British 1st and 6th Airborne Divisions. Once on the ground, and especially under enemy fire, it was imperative that the scooter could be in operation as quickly as possible and paratroops were drilled to remove it from the canister and crucially have it ready for the road in just over ten seconds. Unfortunately, the Welbike was the smallest two-wheeler to enter British military service and in practice would prove to be one of the least successful. It was quite ineffective over the mud-clogged battlefields of Europe and only really showed its true potential during Operation Market Garden, some of the Normandy beach landings and as a handy form of fast shuttle around the numerous overseas air bases. By 1944, airfields in once German occupied areas of Europe were able to safely receive Allied transport aircraft capable of carrying larger payloads

WELBIKE MkII Series 1

W.D Number C5152111 Frame Number 7311
Special Operations Executive
Machine Number 97 of Contract Number S5049
W.D Number Range of C5152014 – C5152413
Frame Number 7214 – 7613 dated 18.11.1942

and the Welbike was rapidly superseded by standard War Office-approved motorcycles more suited to the terrain.

The airdrop two-wheeler concept was not, however, a British idea, having been adopted elsewhere at an earlier stage of the conflicts. Between 1939 and 1941, a pre-War racing driver by the name of Belmondo was tasked with constructing a machine for the Italian army that could again be parachuted into enemy territory. Built in Turin,

the Volugrafo Aermoto was yet another collapsible scooter that most unusually, and unlike its contemporaries, featured twin front and rear wheels (so strictly speaking was a four-wheeler!). Similar to the Welbike, the Aermoto's downfall was its impracticality over rough ground, little helped in no small measure by the quite unnecessary additional wheels. After the War, Societa Volugrafo turned their attention to automobile manufacture with the bizarre Bimbo two-seater. This

Centre: *After the war, some Brockhouse Corgis were used for conveying personnel about military camps with one or two seeing trials aboard aircraft carriers.*

utilised the Aermoto's 125cc 5bhp engine but measured less than 8 ft in length!

One of the most successful scooters proposed for military use was the American-made Eagle. Built by the Cushman Motor Works of Lincoln, Nebraska, it entered service at the start of World War II and carried on in production over a decade after peace was declared. A stable mate was the Cushman Auto Glide Model 53, later renamed the Airborne – yet another vehicle intended for deployment by parachute.

During the 1950s, designer Victor Bouffort came up with the 'scooter in a suitcase' and tried unsuccessfully to secure orders from the French army. His Valmobile could be folded down to fit in a space measuring 27 inches x 14 inches x 24 inches. This micro machine had automatic transmission, a single brake on the rear and a 0.64 gallon fuel tank, and once fully assembled could offer its rider a commendable range of around 165 miles. The carrying case formed the main body of the scooter containing the 50cc 2.8hp engine and was fitted with a rider and pillion passenger seat. Optional extras included a heavy duty or light duty sidecar attachment which perhaps defeated the object! Weighing only 43kg,

the Valmobile's best customer base was in America where it was offered as an optional extra to motor caravan buyers. Another firm, Établissements François,

Ateliers de Construction de Motocycles et Automobiles (or ACMA) faired better with their offering, the TAP 56. This was basically an adapted Piaggio Vespa assembled under licence in Fourchambault. The most noteworthy modification was the attachment of an American manufactured M20 75mm calibre recoilless cannon! As this weapon was almost seven feet in length, accommodating it on the scooter required some radical thinking – one end being located beneath a crude saddle with only a modicum of padding, whilst the other end protruded some three feet forward of the front wheel. In trials, it was found that the 145cc engine struggled to cope with the weight of the M20, ammunition and accompanying paraphernalia such as the tripod required for aiming purposes. Instead, the French Troupes Aéroportées (hence the name TAP), to whom nearly all 56s were assigned operated the scooters in pairs to spread the load. The Troupes Aéroportées found the M20's HEAT 21lbs shells, capable of penetrating 100mm of armour from a maximum distance of 4 miles away, were especially effective against makeshift defences such as pillboxes during the Algerian War.

marketed a similar machine designed specifically for civilian use from 1952.

Whilst the French authorities rejected the Valmobile, a rival firm called

Right: *The Cushman Model 53 not only played a huge role in the rapid advance of Allied forces during World War II, but would also become the unlikely inspiration for both the Lambretta and Vespa. This example is owned by Doug Baldanzi.*

Back on Civvy Street

Although the years 1939 to 1945 saw many of the world's nations embroiled in bloody conflict, not all engineering was geared towards the war effort, and even in countries devastated by fighting, a few hardy souls battled on with their own vehicle designs.

In France there was an acute fuel shortage nationwide and, in an attempt to overcome the situation, Roger Paupe drew up plans for an electric scooter. This was a strange little contraption, sitting low to the road and consisting of a tubular framed box containing a hefty battery pack and two motors, one for an economic jaunt around town and the second to provide a little extra oomph! Paupe was a native of Lyon,

home to Motocyclette New-Map who for a couple of years were tasked with building his scooter in their Avenue Lacassagne works. It could travel up to 50 miles on one charge and had a top speed of 25 miles per hour.

For a range of vehicles mainly built under the austerity measures imposed as a result of World War II, Salsbury Motor Glide scooters continued to be particularly attractive machines. This American business was started by E. Foster Salsbury and Austin Elmore and had commenced trading three years before the conflicts. Motor Glides were characterised by a very narrow body, far slenderer in fact than the hips of the average rider! The road wheels were

Left: *These two fine examples of the American-built Salsbury Motor Glide are owned by Jerry Perkins.*

some of the smallest ever seen on a non-collapsible scooter and could have caused poor handling qualities had it not been for the particularly wide set of handlebars.

In 1938, Motor Glides were the first scooters in the world to feature a continuously variable transmission box. By the late-1940s the production line at the Northrop Aircraft plant in Pomona, California had started building the enormous 320cc side-valve engine 85 Super-Scooter with its aerodynamic nosecone embellished with chrome strips. Measuring almost 8 feet in length the Super-Scooter displayed some peculiar idiosyncrasies including foot-operated accelerator and brake, kick start lever centrally placed beneath the rider's seat, and of course continued using the company's patent automatic transmission. The Salsbury name eventually disappeared off the radar when Northrop decided to concentrate

all efforts on its aviation interests.

In Britain, Lt. Colonel John R.V. Dolphin, the original brains behind the collapsible Welbike was so enamoured with his own concept that when peace finally returned to Europe in 1945, he decided to establish his own business to build a civilian version. A year later, Corgi Motorcycle Co., Ltd was founded in Southport, a town twenty miles north of Liverpool and here a scooter was developed that owed much

to the Welbike's design. It would, however, be stronger and heavier, and as there was no need to pack it into a parachute drop canister, it did not have to be as compact as its military predecessor. Benefiting from a larger capacity fuel tank and with a claimed average fuel consumption of 125 miles per gallon, it had a far greater range than the rider of a Welbike could ever hope for.

When the Corgi first went on

Right: *1954 was the last year of Corgi production. By then, the Mark IV version featured a re-routed exhaust system and a handy luggage rack on the fuel tank. This example was on display at the 2012 South Cerney Steam & Vintage Extravaganza.*

sale, it seems that Dolphin had underestimated its popularity with demand far outstripping supply and in 1947, another Southport company, Brockhouse Engineering, had signed an agreement with Dolphin to manufacture under licence a slightly modified version. Up until then, the Corgi required push starting but a kick start was added for the Mark 2 model and over the next few years, various other changes were made. By 1952, the Brockhouse Corgi featured telescopic front forks and a two speed gearbox as standard. A sidecar could be purchased as an optional extra and to

fully enclose the mechanical elements, a body kit was offered as another after-market product by Corgi's sole concessionaires, Jack Olding & Co., Ltd, of North Audley Street, London.

When production ended in October 1954, nearly 30,000 examples of the Brockhouse Corgi had been built,

most of these being exported to the United States and many sold as the Indian Papoose. As a publicity stunt, one example was ridden from the east coast to the west, but it was not only the Americans who enthused about the Corgi. A healthy following quickly spread to the far reaches of the world

Above: *Although the LE Velocette should strictly be classed as a motorcycle, it bore a number of similarities to Bond's Minibyke and the Belgian Socovel.*

Far Right:
*Whenever a war
ends and there
is a shortage of
raw materials,
there will always
be innovation
in design. The
American Whizzer
tandem was, from
1948, built under
licence in Belgium.*

and an international owners club was instigated not long after production had begun.

A similar machine was the Lefol Aéro-Scoot made in Courbevoie, France although this, at least, had leg shields and proper panelling covering the engine bay, fitted as standard.

Although the Corgi and Aéro-Scoot were compact little machines, they filled the gap between motorcycle and scooter creating a sub-group for a type called the mini-bike.

Another British firm to enter this niche market was the Bond Aircraft & Engineering Co., Ltd of Longridge, Lancashire. In 1949, they unveiled the aptly-named Minibyke, possibly the most extraordinary and unorthodox two-wheeler ever created. A long central barrel sloping from the headstock down towards the back wheel formed not only the main load-bearing component but doubled as the fuel tank. The rest of the frame consisted of a simple web of thin flat steel bars riveted together instead of the usual welded tubing and cradled a 98cc JAP engine. The rigid front forks were also of flat steel bar riveted to an enormous mudguard. This and the almost identical rear mudguard enveloped almost three-quarters of each wheel, a feature that must have proved somewhat inconvenient in the event of a puncture. On each side of the engine were leg shields giving the Minibyke a very distinctive scooter-like appearance. For £55, here was a quirky but useful little machine capable of 50 miles per hour and with a range claimed to be approaching 200 miles per gallon. Within a year or so, the Minibyke was being built with a conventional tube frame and telescopic front forks. Later models followed the German school of design with long and wide rigid bodies from nose to tail. Bond scooters were in production for almost ten years before the company concentrated all efforts on car and commercial vehicle manufacture.

The Socovel range of scooters made in Belgium from 1952 were very similar to the Bond although the engine was fully enclosed behind a rather unattractive flat panel. Taking Bond's idea of the fuel tank forming a stressed member, these 125cc, 150cc and 197cc machines were not popular and the company soon folded.

Italian Chic –
Enter Two Legends

Far Right:
This 1948 Type B shows the open frame and relatively small amount of body panelling typical of early Lambrettas.

The Lambretta story begins in the early-1920s when Ferdinando Innocenti founded Innocenti Società Generale per l'Industria Metallurgica e Meccanica, a steel tube works in the heart of Rome's industrial district. In less than ten years, the business had become so successful that new premises were sought and the whole company was relocated 300 miles north-west to Milan.

It was a period of huge transformation in Italy with a new Fascist government lead by Benito Mussolini taking overall control, and under this totalitarian regime, a structured program of changes were planned for the Italian economy. Public transport was streamlined, large areas of the Pontine Marshes were reclaimed mainly for agricultural use, and as the dark clouds of war gathered on the horizon, the country prepared its military might for the conflicts that would ravage Europe over the next few years. All engineering facilities were requisitioned for the war effort and it was no different for Innocenti's tube factory. The works did not play as important a role during World War II as intended, however, as it was completely destroyed in a bombing raid. Whilst Innocenti was left to survey the rubble, the 6,000 strong workforce were deployed elsewhere.

In an attempt to attack the Germans and Italians on all fronts, British and American forces, many of them crossing the Mediterranean following

the North African campaign, landed on the south shores of Italy and began advancing up the country. Amongst the Macks, GMCs, Whites and of course the ubiquitous Willys Jeeps, the Americans brought with them the diminutive Cushman Airborne scooter. Its simplicity and compactness must have sparked something in Innocenti's imagination as he commissioned aeronautical engineer, Corradino D'Ascanio to design a machine using a similar layout but of more appealing appearance. With the Cushman bearing all the aesthetics of a jerrycan, the task was hardly difficult but Innocenti wanted to be able to manufacture a vehicle that would look chic and attract both male and female buyers.

With D'Ascanio calling upon years of experience working at the Costruzioni Aeronautiche Agusta SpA aviation works, his plans were for a quite revolutionary machine where all working parts placed in a spar frame were fully enclosed beneath smooth and sculpted panelling. Like the Cushman, the small capacity engine would be located in close proximity to the back wheel and in turn this would allow for a step-through riders platform between the handlebar stem and the rider and passenger seats. In essence, this virtually covered the criteria that Innocenti had laid down in that his product should have many of the handling attributes of a motorcycle but without the ever-present risk of oil, mud and road dust soiling the rider's clothing. Innocenti's own expertise, however, had been built upon the fabrication of seamless steel pipes and rejected

D'Ascanio's spar frame in favour of a tubular version. D'Ascanio vehemently disagreed and when Innocenti refused to change his mind, the aeronautical engineer packed his trunk and said goodbye to the organisation altogether, taking his spar-frame plans with him.

Meanwhile...

150 miles to the south, the fighter aircraft manufacturer Piaggio & Co., S.p.A. were also trying to piece together the remains of a business in the aftermath of a bombing raid. The company had suffered a direct hit, not only on their factory in the Tuscany region town of Pontedera, but also at two other sites in Finale Ligure and their original home town, Genoa. The war was coming to a conclusion and the Italian transport infrastructure had been decimated. Road and rail networks were in ruins and any civilian vehicles not commandeered for military use in the desperate struggle to resist defeat could hardly negotiate highways and byways destroyed in many places by heavy shelling. As if the same vision had come to both he and Ferdinando Innocenti, Enrico Piaggio

Far Left: *The MP5 was nicknamed Pato Donald or Paperino by the Piaggio workforce. It was eventually rejected in favour of a design by Corradino D'Ascanio but not before around 100 examples were made. This one is now on display at the Piaggio Museum, Pontedera.*

Right: *The LC was the first Lambretta to feature full body panelling and leg shields. A year after production began, the LD range was introduced and continued in manufacture from 1951 to 1958.*

was looking to address the shortage of vehicles and find a way of getting the Italian population mobile again. Once more it was the American military's scooter, the Cushman Airborne and its civilian predecessor the 50 Series Auto-Glide, that inspired Piaggio to instruct his chief engineers, Vittorio Casini

and Renzo Spolti, to come up with something along similar lines.

The terrible road conditions were obviously becoming a problem and Casini and Spolti decided that the new machine should take the form of a motorcycle with full-length panelling around the German-made Sachs engine

Left: *Johan and Geraldine Schaevorboke of Belgium holidayed around Normandy aboard their Faro Basso Vespa with its amazon-style side-saddle rear seat.*

to prevent mud and grit permeating and damaging the mechanicals. At the front of the bodywork a fairing was incorporated so that the rider would at least benefit from some level of protection as well.

Taking the designation MP5, a prototype was constructed at Biella and, satisfied with their results, the two designers presented it to the boss.

Piaggio was not pleased.

Whether it was the rather unsightly full-length bodywork that dissuaded him or whether it was on hearing that this curious looking contraption had earned the nickname 'Pato Donald' (the Italian translation for Donald Duck), but the

Far Right:
*This late-1950s
Lambretta Li 225
was pictured
waiting at the Red
Funnel Isle of
Wight ferry terminal
in 2012.*

MP5 was swiftly rejected.

Yet instead of castigating Casini and Spolti and sending them scurrying back to the drawing board, Piaggio chose to rethink his ideas and called upon a former associate who he had come to know whilst working in the aeronautical industry. Still smarting from the negative response he had received from Innocenti for his spar-frame scooter, Corradino D'Ascanio came hotfoot from Milan clutching his plans and presented them to the Piaggio team in Pontedera. It was quickly agreed that a prototype should be made and in turn, this was designated the coding MP6.

The MP6 featured D'Ascanio's monocoque spar frame and steel panelling that acted as one stressed member. Beneath the skin, the 98cc engine was horizontally mounted to one side of the rear wheel negating the need for an oily chain drive between the transmission and axle. The axles themselves were an intriguing piece of engineering, both being of stub axle type with suspension again on one side only, allowing if necessary the identical front and rear wheels to be removed and interchanged with a third spare wheel.

When the finished item was presented to Piaggio for his approval, he is reported to have cried, "Sembra una vespa!" or "It looks like a wasp!"

And that folks is how you name a product!

The year was 1946 and with full managerial approval, the newly reconstructed Pontedera factory immediately swung into full production. With this being the first Vespa, appropriately named the 98 after its engine capacity, Piaggio were still feeling their way and a batch of only fifty were completed to test the waters. Later that year, a press launch was arranged ahead of the 98's public unveiling at the Milan Fair.

Across the city and in the former tube works, the air of excitement was not so palpable. Innocenti looked to his surroundings for inspiration to christen his brand new machine. Meandering through the city was the River Lambro and the area in which the new steel tube factory had been relocated in 1931 was Lambrate. It therefore seemed natural to use these as a starting point and the name Lambretta was eventually settled upon. Imaginatively allotted the designation, Type A, the first model bore scant resemblance to its then undisclosed rival

the MP6, only receiving a modicum of panelling simply to protect the rider from muck flicked up from the road surface. It had been several months since D'Ascanio's impassioned departure and with the loss of his designer, Innocenti turned to another aeronautical engineer, Cesare Pallavicino to look at the plans and make any changes. It was considered that the power unit should also be re-evaluated and specialist engineer Pier Luigi Torre was brought in, not only to advise on its final format but to rearrange the layout of the production line in order to maximise factory output so that large-scale manufacture could commence as soon as possible.

The 125cc motor and fuel tank

LITTLE BOOK OF **SCOOTERS**

Above: *A beautifully restored Vespa 90 Super Sprint of the mid-1960s.*

were left exposed (the latter placed directly below the rider's seat), but a handy storage box could neatly be accommodated beneath the pillion passenger's seat as an option.

A full year after Piaggio's Vespa hit the high street, the Lambretta was ready for its own public unveiling. During that intervening time, 2,500 Vespas had left the Pontedera works, a figure that would quadruple for 1948, double again for 1949 and reach an astonishing output of 60,000 by the turn of the decade. The success was helped by an increase in engine capacity and a sports model called the 98 Corsa joining the range. In ten years, the Vespa had gone from a rejected idea by the people at

Innocenti to one of the best-selling vehicles on Italian roads with over one million examples having sold to happy customers by the mid-1950s.

In contrast, the comparatively gangly Lambretta had not faired so well and it was not until the introduction of the Type LC with its fully-enclosed mechanicals that sales began to significantly catch up.

With the simplicity of design, ease of maintenance and value for money, Vespas and Lambrettas equated to the ideal transport solution for both developed and underdeveloped nations of the world and instead of paying duty on each imported machine, satellite factories and agencies were set up amongst such diverse cultures as America, Brazil, Spain and India.

One of the earliest companies to take advantage of the concept was traditional large motorcycle manufacturer, Douglas (Kingswood) Engineering Ltd. Three years before their Bristol works took up the mantle of Britain's premier scooter mass producer, Douglas were on the verge of bankruptcy. It was only when Managing Director, Claude McCormack, had seen for himself how popular the Vespa was whilst on

a family vacation in Italy that an idea formulated as to how the west-country business could be saved. Between 1951 and 1965, 126,230 Douglas-Vespas were completed before a neighbouring organisation, Westinghouse Brake & Signal Co., Ltd bought them out. In 1959 Piaggio, who in that year were bought out by FIAT SpA, started sending an almost complete knock-down scooter kit of its 152L2 model to Bristol for final assembly; prior to that, all parts for the Douglas-Vespa were entirely fabricated on British soil with the iconic teardrop bodywork outsourced to the Midlands-based panel makers, Pressed Steel.

Douglas were not the only company who approached Piaggio to build Vespas. MISA in Belgium, the Madrid-based firm MotoVespa, and Hoffman and Messerschmitt in Germany ensured D'Ascanio's design attracted fans right across Europe. Not to be outdone, Innocenti sold licences to SIT in France, NSU of Neckarsulm, Germany and Servata in Spain to build its Lambretta.

Towards the end of the 1960s, history was beginning to repeat itself and demand for scooters declined exactly as it had done forty years earlier. Once

Right: *The 2011 Lambretta LN125, made in Italy and Taiwan.*

again it was the compact family car that brought the industry to its knees as it had become fashionable to own a FIAT 500, 2CV or one of the many bubble-cars on offer such as the idiosyncratic Messerschmitt KR175 three-wheeler or its fellow countryman, the four-wheeled Isetta. Before agreeing with Italian firm ISO to build their peculiar Isetta which one entered via a door over the front bumper, management at BMW had considered building a scooter called the R10. It seems this model only reached the prototype stage until being shelved in favour of the Isetta. It is interesting to note that several years earlier, Piaggio had gone in the other direction and tried their hand at micro car construction with the 400 coupé. This enjoyed a little more success than the R10, however, and from 1957 to 1961, nearly 35,000 examples of this 2+2 seater four-wheeler left the Pontedera works.

But for the late-'60s, it was the Suez Crisis that was threatening European fuel supplies and, with the future of large gas-guzzling cars beginning to look uncertain, sales of the BMC Mini were particularly on the up. Indeed it was the Mini that would eventually

cause the Lambretta production line to finally grind to a halt. The factory in Milan had for a while been assembling a distinctively Italian-styled take on Alec Issigonis's most celebrated creation under licence and the association was further cemented in 1971 when the recently-formed British Leyland Motor Corporation assumed control of the Innocenti Group. The rapid expansion of BLMC's empire had, however, been ill-advised and with finances spread too thinly, the decision was made to make cuts – the Milanese scooter factory becoming one of a number of casualties.

Whilst the situation had become decidedly bleak in Italy, Scooter India Ltd (SIL), a government funded organisation, grasped the opportunity

and in 1972 bought all Lambretta production rights ending its European association for the next forty years. Although the Lambretta name was retained for SIL's export market, models intended for sale on Indian soil adopted the Vijay brand.

Elsewhere in India, LML launched a retro-styled 150cc two-stroke scooter called the Stella – not to be confused with an unorthodox French machine of the 1950s. Whilst the Indian Stella enjoyed considerable success when exported to the United States, floor space at the Kanpur factory was shared with a Vespa P-Series assembly line allowing Piaggio a foothold in the lucrative Indian market. Both the Stella and its Vespa stable-mate shared many

Above: In 1972, SIL bought all rights to make Lambrettas. Although export models such as this one retained the Lambretta name, on Indian soil they were marketed as the Vijay.

Above: *This Vespa lookalike is in fact a Star, manufactured in India by LML.*

Right: *The Vespa-based Chetak was yet another scooter made in India, this time by Bajaj Auto Ltd of Pune, Maharashtra.*

components to economise on pattern making but in later years, examples sold on the American continent were specially fitted with a four-stroke engine to comply with California's strict emissions legislation.

Another Indian company that signed an agreement with Piaggio to start building Vespas was Bajaj Auto Ltd. Although this might be an unfamiliar name in Britain, Bajaj's fortunes slowly improved throughout the 1980s to the extent that by the following decade, they had become nearly the largest scooter manufacturer in the world, second only to the mighty Piaggio Group, and with an annual output of 700,000 machines! The most popular models were the Chetak, Legend, Priya and Super, the first two continuing in production right up to 2009.

By contrast, the number of two-wheeled transport built by SIL gradually declined and in 1997 it was decided to end manufacture of scooters in order to concentrate on three-wheeler production.

Left: *Lets hope there is only one light dipping switch!*

Imitation is the Sincerest Form of Flattery

Both Lambretta and Vespa were not without their imitators and, especially in Italy, the chic and proven fully-enclosed scooter concept was taken as a blueprint for others to emulate.

The concerted efforts of MV, Palmieri & Gulinelli, San Cristoforo, and Società Italiana Motoscooters (SIM), for example, did not exactly hit the mark but the influences were plain to see. MV's Ovunque model was quite obviously a clone of the early open-frame Lambrettas whilst Palmieri & Gulinelli chose to endow their late-1950s Vespa-inspired models with large spoked wheels giving them a very individualistic though not entirely convincing appearance.

San Cristoforo, a close neighbour of Innocenti had, after the War, bought out the Gianca business and moved all proceedings from Monza to Milan. Taking Gianca's quirky but nevertheless popular Nibbio as a starting point, they re-designed the panelling to be more in line with Vespa profiling and re-launched it under the San Cristoforo brand. Instead of improving the Nibbio's looks, the new version that would eventually become the Simonetta sat awkwardly on the road and the body curves were not as fluid as their more successful counterparts.

As for SIM, their efforts looked

IMITATION IS THE SINCEREST FORM OF FLATTERY

more like a clockwork tin-plate toy than a serious attempt at scooter production. Definition of all curves, louvers and grille covers seemed to have been over-emphasised resulting in a chunky but clumsy model that, alas, could not last the distance and by the 1960s had disappeared from the scene.

Aermacchi, Agrati-Garelli, Motobi and Paglianti on the other hand seemed to have a basic grasp as to what looked cool and were able to successfully translate this understanding into their products. Aermacchi were yet another casualty of World War II, required under the terms of the Allied-imposed peace treaty to switch from their former occupation of aircraft development and provide alternative employment for its skilled engineers. In 1950, they turned their attention to the light two-wheeler and over the following decade created a range of successful and occasionally not so successful models. In their twilight years, Aermacchi finally seemed to hit on the right formula and assembled arguably some of the most attractive scooters to come out of Italy. With the downturn in scooter sales during

the 1960s, however, their golden years proved short-lived.

Agrati-Garelli built no-nonsense machines with clean lines and attractive colour schemes and from 1958 to the mid-1960s were noteworthy adversaries to the larger corporations.

Pesaro, a town in the Marche region of Italy and famed as the home of motorcycling marque Benelli, was assured its place in scooter history when one of the Benelli family, Giuseppe, founded Motobi. Unlike his brothers, he had recognised the merits of the Vespa and from 1956, the growing choice of scooters on offer included the attractive Motobi Catria. This differed from the Vespa in that the engine was mounted in the frame between the front and rear wheels necessitating a tunnel to be included in the body panelling. Although there was still a relatively low step-through, this meant that the Catria's foot-boards were divided and placed either side of the bike. With a smooth four-stroke 175cc motor and Earles-type front forks providing superior braking and handling, the Catria was an altogether more accomplished piece of engineering than many of its contemporaries.

Very similar to the Catria but perhaps not quite as aerodynamic was the sturdy little 48cc Cip made 150 miles to the north in Dosson di Treviso and just outside Venice by Paglianti.

One of the most successful models whose lines mimicked those of the Vespa was built, not in Italy, but in Bielefield, Germany, by Dürkoppwerke AG. The Dürkopp Diana, lasted in production from 1953 to 1959 and took the Vespa design to a new level of luxury and quality workmanship. Contemporary motorcycling magazines were especially impressed by the excellent standard of finish that suitably complimented the model's equally commendable handling capabilities. Each of these lovely little machines was fitted with a fan-cooled 194cc engine coupled to a four-speed gearbox. They should have enjoyed a longer life but at £214 for a new one, the asking price was just a little too steep for the average pocket.

It was not until 1957 that members of the Russian population could purchase a home-grown but blatant clone of the iconic Vespa when Vyatsko-Polianskiy Machinostroital'niy Zavod (VPMZ)

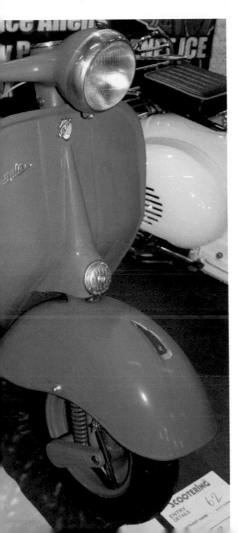

brought out the Vjatka VP-150. Built in the Siberian town of Vyatskie Polyany, the Vjatka was sold all over the USSR. Because some of these communities were so isolated from the outside world, it was reported that when they finally saw an actual bona-fide Vespa, they were convinced it was a copy of the VP-150! There were, however, subtle differences between the Italian and Russian models, the most noticeable being that the VP-150 had larger diameter wheels and weighed substantially more due to the thicker metal used for the pressed steel panelling.

The Vjatka was not the only scooter introduced in the USSR in 1957 and 500 miles away, the first examples of the T.200 were leaving the Tula Motorzikly Zavod (TMZ) factory in Tula.

It would be unfair to label these other concerns as 'pretenders' because the number of individual sales certainly ensured their place in scooter history, but with none of them lasting much more than ten years apiece, their popularity were always going to be overshadowed by the two main contenders, the godfathers of the scootering world, Lambretta and Vespa.

Right: *A nice example of the Vjatka V-150M which went on sale in 1966 as a direct successor to the VP-150.*

Электрон

LITTLE BOOK OF **SCOOTERS**

French Fancies and British Eccentricity

Outside of Italy, the main European centre of scooter production during the early 1950s was France. The French have always displayed a style and flair all of their own and although it could be said that a number of the country's scooter designs took initial inspiration from their Italian counterparts, there was certainly a marked difference between the products of the two nations.

Models like the Motobécane Type M and the exquisite Paloma Vispetta could hold their own against imported scooters from across the border. More and more manufacturers were offering practically identical designs but marketed under various branding. 'Badge engineering', as it was known, was a clever ploy giving customers a seemingly wider choice of scooters. The distinctive Alcyon Paris–Nice with its beak-like front mudguard, for example, was identical to a scooter sold by Mors Speed and it was hard to tell the Automoto SA3, FMC S.555 and Peugeot S.55 apart from each other. They all, however, enjoyed encouraging sales but would never be able to match the interest in Piaggio's Vespa.

Probably the most successful of all French scooter producers was Peugeot who, in leaner periods, were able to fall back on profits made from its car industry. They first entered the market in 1953 and for the next twenty years advertised a pleasant range of machines under the Peugeot as well as its subsidiary

brand names. Factory output was largely concentrated on car manufacture during the 1970s and only in the mid-1980s did they once again consider scooter sales as a sustainable form of income.

Throughout the following decade, the Peugeot catalogue included the aggressive looking 50cc Speedake and Speedfight which were in direct competition with Aprilia's SR, the Malaguti Phantom, Piaggio's Zip and the Yamaha Aerox. In recent times the 125cc, 250cc, 400cc and 500cc Satelis touring models, initially launched in 2006, took styling cues from the company's 407 car.

From the sublime to the ridiculous and every now and then, a French

machines that were cheap to buy, had a reasonable level of reliability and were very easy to maintain.

Quite what the Courbevoie-based Vélosolex concern were trying to achieve when they began building the Micron in 1967, however, is anyone's guess but if there was ever a Black & Decker Workmate equivalent in the scootering world, then this awful looking thing was it. Harking back to the days of the 1920s Auto-Ped, the designer chose to locate the engine directly below the headstock so that motor steered with the front wheel. The frame was made up of crude flat steel plates bolted together and the only form of suspension for the entire contraption was represented by a single spring below the saddle. Whoever designed it failed to include pedals to fire up the 49cc engine with push starting remaining the only other option. In the form, it had to be categorised under French law as a motorcycle meaning that the rider required a full licence to operate one. To make matters worse, the Micron had a top speed in excess of 19 miles per hour, not exactly the sort of performance to get the pulses racing! Nevertheless, over 4,000 examples found buyers too daft to search the market for an alternative.

Left: *The utilitarian Velosolex Micron took rudimentary design to the extreme.*

model would emerge that, by its own grand unveiling, could only have been met with derision. Understandably, very few of these made it into serious mass production and in some cases should have remained no more than a prototype if not a drawing on the back of a cigarette packet! Yet some of these bizarre creations found particular use amongst the French population living in outlying rural districts. This was because these scooters were plain, unadorned of fancy bodywork and, possessing a certain ruggedness, could cope with the gruelling workaday rigours of farm life.

AGF, Aubier-Dunne, Carley and Paul Vallee are just some of the many firms that built no-nonsense open-frame

Equally unappealing was the Babymoto which had been made in Saint-Etienne several years before. This definitely had a scooter air about it with leg shields, step-through foot-board and engine placed below the rider's seat. At best the Babymoto was functional rather than attractive with its rather austere square-edged panelling nestling amongst a quite separate tubular frame.

The Babymoto's most unorthodox feature was a trailing link suspension on the front wheel with a central hydraulic damper and two spring outriggers which, at the very least, must have made for an unusual riding experience.

A number of French manufacturers chose to incorporate large motorcycle-type wheels and pedal starters so that many of the models took on a distinctive

moped appearance. With the size and specification of some of these machines, it was sometimes difficult to pigeon hole them in either scooter, moped or lightweight motorcycle camps which lead to the coining of the term 'scooter-bike'. Bernet, Cazenave, Jonghi, Libéria and Peugeot were just some of the firms adopting this look and although not as chic as the Italian profile all-enclosed scooters, they still made up a good percentage of localised sales. Out of all

of these, the Ninon was perhaps most closely related to the scooter with a very low slung frame, centrally-placed 49cc Poulain engine and a one-piece leg-shield that swept down into the foot-board that also acted as a protective tray beneath the two-speed motor. The Ninon's low centre of gravity, drum brakes and front forks mounted on rubber bushes meant it was a surprisingly nice machine to ride, yet did not attract many takers.

Across the English Channel, Britain

was fielding a number of scooter manufacturers, all vying for a slice of the European market. Long-forgotten marques such as Ambassador, Dunkley, Phœnix and Sun had all put in an appearance in the post-war rush to encourage a population tired of rationing and austerity measures to get back out on the road again. With growing foreign competition especially from Japan, however, practically all had disappeared again by the mid-1960s.

It was a familiar story for DKR, a firm set up at Pendeford Airfield near Wolverhampton by directors of the Willenhall Motor Radiator Company, Barry Day and Noah Robinson, and Cyril Kieft who was probably best known for the construction of centrally-driven three seater sports cars, one of which won the 2-litre Class at the 1954 Sebring 12-Hours.

Above: *Okay, so it is neither a French or British machine, but this German-built Simson Schwalbe (meaning Swallow) was typical of the large wheel scooters emerging from Europe during the 1960s.*

Far Right: *The Velocette Viceroy had a 250cc opposed twin-cylinder engine and fuel tank encased behind the leg-shield and in front of the step-through, with shaft drive to the rear wheel.*

DKR scooters were a strange and not altogether attractive breed that combined the German 'Kolossal'-type rigid mudguard/leg shield front end (described in greater detail in the next chapter) with a less cumbersome rear end of a style more in line with Italian thinking. The catalogue mainly consisted of four versions, the 147cc Dove introduced in 1957, the 148cc Pegasus DeLuxe, the 197cc Defiant DeLuxe, and the 250cc Manx. The last three were launched a year after the Dove and all DKRs were fitted with Villiers single cylinder units apart from the top-of-the-range Manx which had a twin-cylinder two-stroke engine producing speeds of up to 70mph. The high profile parrot-shaped nose cone concealing the fuel tank on all models would today have particular 'retro' appeal, but in the 1950s proved less attractive to the buying public. At the beginning of the following decade, this design was revised with the Capella range and the fuel tank was moved to a more conventional location under the seat.

The James SC.1 on the other hand really had something of the Vespa about it and was an altogether more pleasing machine. It first went on sale in 1960 and had a 150cc single-cylinder engine mounted horizontally under the footboard meaning that it was not only a nicely balanced machine in looks but in handling as well.

Like DKR, another Midlands firm, Sun, had started inauspiciously with a less than successful design in the Geni. Right from the off, its centrally-placed 98cc engine was just not powerful enough to carry the weight of the full-length tunnel-type bodywork as well as a rider and passenger, and only two years into production, a new model shamelessly called the Wasp was introduced. This followed Vespa practice with an improved layout and step-through footboard. Engine capacity was increased and the dual seating unit hid from view the larger 148cc or 173cc units mounted adjacent to the rear wheel.

Jules Verne Would Have Been Proud

During the six years of World War II, considerable advances in jet and rocket propulsion were made so that by the early 1950s, the possibilities of space flight were verging on reality. Interest in what lay 'out there' beyond the Earth's atmosphere had gradually increased over the previous twenty years and the artists who penned such heroes as Buck Rogers, Flash Gordon and Dan Dare brought the rocket age to life with futuristic space craft, laser guns and fantastic representations in aerodynamic design.

But these wonderful flights of fancy were not only confined to the pages of popular children's comics; the automobile industry too had started to adopt a kind of flair that would last right through to the late-1960s. Cars especially of American origin, had for a long time been adorned with fins, chrome and torpedo or bullet-shaped detailing and European manufacturers who had initially been slow to catch on were using these elements more and more in their own products.

These ultra-modern styling exercises transferred particularly well to the panel-heavy qualities of the diminutive scooter and some wonderful creations began to appear particularly in the early 1950s.

In Germany there developed a vogue for the 'kolossal'-type scooter characterised by a rather bulbous body, rigid from nose to tail, so that instead of

the leading mudguard steering with the front wheel, the wheel turned within a shell that was either fixed to or sculpted as part of the leg shield assembly. The wide overhang on both sides meant that the wheels were almost hidden from view giving an overall impression that its occupants were riding on a large hovering shoe! The idea was fundamentally to provide better protection for the riders and a number of firms took up the challenge including Bastert, Kroboth, Maïco and Pantherwerke, with most

choosing to market their models along the lines of a 'car on two wheels'.

Between 1950 and 1955, Maïco of Pfäffingen-Tübingen sold the Maïco-Mobil. In an attempt to address irregular weight distribution suffered by some of the contemporary models, Maïco chose to position the engine half way between the seat and handlebar stem, with the fuel tank just in front. This meant that the Mobil had superior balance over a machine that had most of the weight located on the rear wheel which, in

Above: The Maïco Mobil was one of several scooter models that were known as the 'Kolossal'-type due to their size and the enormous amount of body panelling.

LITTLE BOOK OF **SCOOTERS**   85

Right: *Another model by Maico was the Maicoletta. Built between 1954 and 1966, a choice of 174cc, 247cc or 277cc engines were available.*

some cases, could cause the front end to wheelie especially when pulling away on an incline. The Mobil's vast expanse of panelling included a tunnel with a removable cover to access the 150cc, 175cc and later 200cc unit. On the underside was a tray to protect the engine, four-speed gearbox and chain drive. The rear axle was attached to the frame via a leaf-sprung swing arm while twin-telescopic front forks provided suspension to the front – both forks being sited on one side so that the stub-axle mounted wheels could be easily interchanged with the spare. The latter was encased within a barrel-back that also contained lockable pannier compartments either side of the rear wheel. With all that bodywork and heavy suspension adding to the load, the Mobil required a dual fan-assisted cooling system to prevent overheating.

Equally impressive was the almost identical Motorroller made in Bavaria by Fahrzeug und Maschinenbau Gustav Kroboth, a company that salvaged World

Left: *The Tourist was made by Heinkel Flugzeugwerke from 1953 to 1965 with over 100,000 examples leaving the Karlsruhe factory, Germany.*

War II military vehicles for a source of raw materials. The only major disparity between Motorroller and the Maïco-Mobil was a lack of panniers at the rear. Unfortunately the production life of this model only lasted for three years.

Pantherwerke's Karat again displayed wide protective legshields for its occupants but was endowed with a distinctively attractive and more streamlined body. The Mobil, Motorroller and Karat were all available with optional windscreen attachments but even these could not boost struggling sales. By the mid-1950s all had but disappeared from their respective catalogues to be replaced by more conventional models.

Automobile influences were certainly evident on the Bastert Einspur-Auto. Designed by Frenchman Louis Lepoix it featured chrome bumpers, front and rear directional indicators, and a dashboard with dials, switches and an illuminated display that showed the rider which gear he was in. Around 1,200 examples left Helmut Bastert's Bielefeld factory

Right: *IWL (Industriewerke Ludwigsfelde) was founded in East Germany in 1952. The Berlin model was introduced in 1959.*

between 1952 and 1956.

It was not only the Germans who liked the 'car on two wheels' idea and as the last of the Einspur–Autos were rolling off the Bastert production line, twins Paul and Pierre Roussey were planning to launch a similar machine in Dijon, France. All major components were carried on a central tube and cradled below this was a horizontal 170cc unit of the Roussey brother's own

design – a luxury this small firm could ill-afford. For ease of maintenance, the entire body shell from the headstock back could be lifted, hinging on an extension of the frame behind the rear wheel. Development from prototype to a model sufficiently ready for public consumption took three years yet, in the end, this gestation period proved longer than the production run.

Only a stones throw across town,

Terrot, decided to launch its own take on the scooter. Originally a maker of proprietary engines, the factory was set up as a satellite works to a main engineering plant in Cannstatt, Germany. Throughout both World Wars, Terrot had enjoyed good patronage from the French Army, first for their 500cc twin-cylinder motorcycles and from 1942 additional 350cc, 750cc and sidecar outfits. Although their 1951 VMS was

not as aerodynamic as the 'kolossal'-type machines, it was nevertheless of very modern appearance with attractive curves and touches of chrome. Taking advantage of 'badge-engineering' to allow potential buyers something of a wider choice, the VMS was also made as the Magnat-Debon S1, identical in all but name. When it first appeared, the VMS was a single-seater model with an, at best, adequate 98cc engines located

under the riding position. When a pillion seat was later added, the motor struggled to cope with the added weight especially if the passenger was on the large size and a 125cc version called the VMS1 joined the range. Later still, Terrot and Magnat-Debon scooters were upgraded again to include a pre-selector gearbox. The VMS and S1 would be the first in a considerable line of Terrot scooters, mopeds and low-powered motorcycles that for the next ten years would vie with big guns Piaggio and Lambretta for a slice of the lightweight two-wheeler market. In 1958, the French branch of

the company was bought by motoring giants Peugeot who, in a program of sweeping changes closed the factory only four years later ending Terrot's legacy.

Meanwhile Cyclemaster of Byfleet, Surrey, had commenced building what respected motorcycle historian, Bob Currie, would later describe as "the worst scooter ever perpetuated"! Conceived by an Italian designer, the Piatti was a tubby little thing incorporating some rather unorthodox features including a rigid body encompassing the front mudguard, 7 inch wheels and a dual seat that perched high on a height-adjustable stem. Like the P.P. Roussey, the Piatti's single-cylinder engine was laid flat in a tunnel but drove the rear wheel via twin chains. An identical machine was also made under licence in Belgium by D'leteren but with its overall appearance not unlike something one would see on a fairground ride and providing questionable street credibility, few were ever sold.

In stark contrast to these bulky looking machines, the Bernadet E.51, HMW Bambi and the Marinavia Marinella were striking little works of art with more than a touch of futurism and would not have looked out of place in the hands of the Jetsons or the Mekon! The Marinella, especially, could have been a thing of pure science fiction had a prototype not appeared in the late 1940s, and it is such a shame that the model was not developed further.

In the mid-1950s, the Czechoslovakian firm, CZ, announced the Cezeta. This had a distinctively unique profile with a large headlight acting as a focal point from which the bodywork tapered back in marked straight lines, accentuated by a two-tone colour scheme. The long fixed mudguard over the front wheel, protected by a small chrome bumper

Left: Another beautifully restored machine, a CZ Cezeta with matching PAV single-wheel trailer, both made in the former Czechoslovakia.

JULES VERNE WOULD HAVE BEEN PROUD

Far Right:
*Celebrated
American
motorcycle
manufacturer
Harley Davidson
only ever
produced one
scooter model -
the Topper.*

extension, contained the fuel tank and was fitted with a luggage rack. At the rear a useful locker box lay beneath the dual seat with a spare wheel attached at an angle to the very back end. The Cezeta was also made under licence as the La Bohème by neighbouring company, Jawa. A three-wheeled version of the Cezeta called the 505 was launched in 1961. Only the front mudguard and mechanicals were features shared with its scooter stable mate as the 505's driver was shielded from inclement weather within an all-enclosed cab whilst the rear load carrying space was made available in a number of guises including flat bed, drop side or van.

Despite the title of this chapter, there is one scooter that Jules Verne would probably not have been proud of. In fact, it has been very difficult to find an appropriate place to include the rather boxy Topper which was the surprise model of 1959, not least because it was built by famous big bore motorcycle manufacturer, Harley-Davidson. Where European styling embraced Italian-inspired fluid lines, sweeping curves and teardrop detailing, the Topper was a mass of straight edges and sharp corners. Not entirely unattractive, its

pressed steel fairing, foot board and front mudguard as well as the fibre-glass body were certainly futuristic. When World War II had come to an end, various aspects of the Germany's industry were offered to other countries as war reparations. Amongst the many parts given over to the Americans were drawings of the DKW RT 125 which were subsequently passed on to Harley-Davidson. Russia and Britain also took copies of the drawings and from 1948, BSA made the Bantam whilst Moskovskiy Mototsikletniy Zavod built the MM3, both models based on the German RT 125 design.

Under the Topper's shell was a 165cc single-cylinder 2-stroke unit, about as far-removed from the usual 1,000cc and 1,200cc V-twin machines coming out of Milwaukee at that time. It was felt that air passing beneath the scooter would be enough to cool the engine so no fan was included and, unfortunately, many examples suffered from overheating.

What diehard Harley-Davidson fans must have thought when the Topper was publicly unveiled is anyone's guess but for six years, the Topper allowed the company to successfully tap into the American scooter market.

A Racing Pedigree

Far Right: *The
Vespa 98 Corsa
was purpose-built
for circuit racing
and could reach
speeds in excess
of 60mph. This
machine is on
display at the
Piaggio Museum,
Pontedera.*

In every field of motoring, there will always be a group of enthusiasts who strive to push the boundaries, testing the vehicles beyond the capabilities for which they were originally designed and taking them to their very limits.

Some of the first forays were in fact by Piaggio and Innocenti, both companies realising that one of the best ways to publicise and boost scooter sales, which at that time was still a relatively rare type of transport, was to win competitive events. In 1949 at the Genoa Circuit a Vespa 125, known as the 'telaio in lega' because of its alloy frame, was ridden by company test rider and nominated works racer, Dino Mazzoncini, who overcame the only opposition which just happened to be a Lambretta! Piaggio went one step further, however, and decided that even greater media attention could be garnered not by racing against other competitors, but by beating the clock and contest land speed records.

A year after Mazzoncini's victory against Piaggio's arch rivals, another specially-prepared Vespa decked out with extraordinary streamlined bodywork took part in a mammoth attempt on a whole host of records. On the 7th April 1950, three of Piaggio's best riders, Castiglioni, Otello Spadoni and Dino Mazzoncini took it in turns around the Montlhery circuit in France, and between them

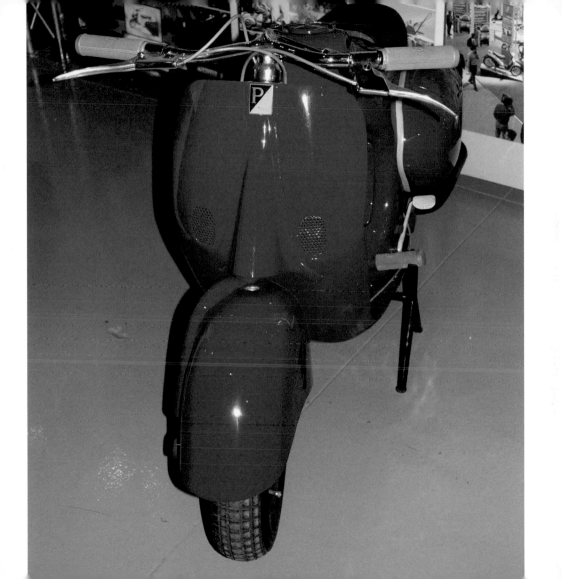

surpassed all public expectations by raising the bar in no less than seventeen different categories. With a top speed of 85 miles per hour, records for the 1 Hour, 100 Miles, 500 Miles and 1,000 Kilometres tumbled and over a marathon 10-hour slog, a total of 1,059 miles were covered ensuring public confidence in the reliability of Piaggio's products.

For 1951, Piaggio called on the Vespa's original designer, Corradino D'Ascanio to create a machine that could attack the standing kilometre record. The result was the 'Siluro' (Torpedo), a substantially more aerodynamic machine than the Montlhery bike with a wonderfully sculpted slippery body. Powered by a water-cooled horizontally opposed twin-cylinder unit with a separate carburettor per cylinder and a double drive-shaft to the rear wheels, the little 125cc engine was tuned to produce a power output of 17.2 brake horsepower at 9,500 revs per minute. Ten months after the successful Montlhery record attempts, the Piaggio team triumphed again as Dino Mazzoncini propelled the Vespa Siluro past all previous standing kilometre benchmarks with a time of 21.4 seconds and an average speed of 106.3 miles per hour.

With large-scale mass-production only becoming reality after World War II, the scooter community were naturally latecomers to motor sport. The first contests were amateur affairs developed through club meets and gatherings. They began as impromptu reliability trials where participants attempted to navigate specially laid out courses with riders being judged on their performance over and around a number of obstacles. The nature of the trials, however, only allowed for one entrant (or pairing if aboard a sidecar outfit) to come under scrutiny at any given time and it was clear that a great many competitors and spectators alike wanted something a little more exciting to entertain them on a Saturday or Sunday afternoon.

Initially they raced with their larger motorcycle counterparts and for a while could hold their own, but as motorcycles became faster and more powerful, the scooter struggled to keep pace and were eventually designated their own series. Rules and regulations were laid down by the Federation of British Scooter Clubs (FoBSC)

who, under the guidance of the Auto Cycle Union, proceeded to organise and govern the meetings as well as provide teams of marshalling staff at various circuits and trials. Whilst many club members steadfastly voted to preserve the social elements of their respective organisations, others broke away and formed their own groups specifically set up to assist one another on technical matters and to campaign their machines in competitive events. Unlike other motoring disciplines, women, albeit in their own classes, were able to race and share centre stage taking honours and plaudits on a level footing with the men.

By the early-1970s, road-racing had a substantial following and perhaps the most popular rounds of the British Championships were held during the Isle of Man Scooter Week ensuring a good number of entries and a large audience. With a crowd full of potential buyers watching proceedings, racing became the ultimate advertising platform and the sport was attracting participation from some of the major manufacturers who were fielding their own works riders. The week encompassed a variety of

Far Left: *Piaggio entered ten Sports Vespas in the 26th Be Giorni Internazionale of 1951, with nine riders winning gold medals. No.94 was ridden by Giuseppe Cau.*

competitions such as hill climbs, night trials and sand races, and although it was the road racing that provided the main interest, the same riders could choose to take part in a number of different events.

One of the spectacles of the whole occasion would be the mass ensemble, consisting of thousands of scooters loaded to the gunnels with tents, sleeping bags and holdalls full of clothes, descending on Liverpool each year to board the Isle of Man Steam Packet ferry ahead of the week. For the next few days, the island would reverberate to convoys of Vespas, Lambrettas and other contemporary models, touring the roads, seeing the sights and on their way to watch the action on the Ballaugh and Druidale circuits. Of course the start of the return journey which, for many, represented a long and arduous ride home, was equally impressive as scooterists from clubs nationwide once again gathered on the port side at Douglas to head back to mainland Britain.

Over the years, several names became prominent within the rankings including Pete Chapman, Nev Frost, Doug May, Ron Moss,

Far Left: *It doesn't get much better than this! Four legends together at a 1952 Goodwood meeting – racing drivers Harry Schell and Peter Collins with Stirling Moss aboard an early Vespa.*

Geoff Stephens and the Frankland and Ronald brothers. The women were represented by the likes of Bev Flannagan, Elizabeth Smollen, June Stirrup and Ann Weir, and having dominated their individual categories as solo riders, Frost and Flannagan became a force to be reckoned with when they paired up for sidecar events.

In the years leading up to the end of the 20th Century, another body called the National Scooter Sport Association

evolved to allow club level competitors from across the country to race in major championships. In time the NSSA and the FoBSC merged to form the British Scooter Sport Organisation so that all contests large or small

could be overseen by one professional governing body, providing coverage and results from events nationwide, and above all ensuring that essential health and safety requirements were met at every venue.

A New Era

Far Right: *1964 Honda C50.*

Whilst the 1950s and '60s proved boom years for European and especially Italian scooter manufacturers, later decades belonged to the Japanese. Honda's C100 had already sold in their millions and although much of the company's output concentrated on high-powered motorcycles including the highly successful CB750 and enormous Gold Wing models, Honda were able to introduce a new breed of scooter during the 1980s. To satisfy the next generations, the CN250 Helix, a scooter designed for touring, joined the line-up in 1686. The Helix was the first of what would eventually become the maxi-scooter class, large machines that could cope with long-distance journeys and have the engine capacity on a par with mid-size motorcycles to cope with heavier loads.

In time, Honda's main rivals, Aprilia, Gilera, Piaggio, Suzuki and Yamaha all followed Honda's lead and unveiled their own large touring models, and four-stroke engines became a standard option across the board.

In 1996, Piaggio celebrated fifty years as a scooter manufacturer and in those five decades of production, more than fifteen million Vespas had been sold worldwide. But over the next ten years, Piaggio's financial position became decidedly precarious. Ill-advised investment had sent the company into the red and only a rescue plan by entrepreneur, Roberto

Colaninno, and a reorganisation of the assembly line would see the famous brand survive and continue trading into the next century. Under Colaninno's guardianship, working conditions within the factory were vastly improved and a series of new projects saw the company begin to recover. With governments around the world looking to stem the damage that their industries could be causing to the Earth's ozone layer, legislation was instigated in order to limit the average levels of harmful carbon monoxide emissions over a every vehicle manufacturer's entire range. Established firms with a long tradition of building petrol-engined machines were obliged to introduce alternative fuels to reduce

Left: *Scootering 1980s style – an example of the ubiquitous Honda Melody Mini.*

Above: *The exoskeleton Dragster range was made by Italjet of Bologna and sold on the UK market from 1998 to 2003.*

emission figures and in 2004, the world's first petrol-electric scooter was launched at Pontedera.

As the 1990s came to a close and the new Millennium dawned, there seemed to be a distinct desire amongst designers within the motoring establishment to celebrate vehicles from the past. Whilst many concept cars unveiled to motor show visitors largely embraced fresh thinking, a significant number began to exhibit styling that daringly harked back

to that glorious post-war era of the 1950s and '60s. It is particularly the case in the United Kingdom, Belgium and Holland that the public have always been able to look back with sentimental nostalgia to an age when Britain and its European counterparts were still respected and regarded as world leaders of engineering.

The car most people would probably associate with early-1950s film star James Dean, for example, was the mid-engined 550 Spider and Porsche had obviously taken inspiration from their iconic little sports car as a starting point for the Boxster. Fellow German manufacturer, Volkswagen, was already constructing a modern version of the Beetle and had also built a concept camper van that

emulated the lines of the split screen Type 2. BMW responded with an up-to-date albeit much larger incarnation of the Mini and had even taken elements of the 507 open two-seater sports car to create the Z3, Z4 and Z8 roadsters. Companies were looking back to their most popular sellers and attempting to replicate the spirit of the original whilst at the same time incorporating advanced levels of technology, road-holding, specification and safety requirements in line with other vehicles in their respective catalogues.

In scootering circles, it was felt that the classic teardrop lines typical of the 1950s Vespa and its contemporaries should be revisited. The scooter was enjoying something of a revival with much of the credit going to regular television appearances as part of the scene in and around the Formula One pit lane. Alongside off-road machines such as the high riding Honda Ruckus and the sports models with their latticework exoskeleton frame, exposed engines and suspension, and aggressive chisel-edged looks, there emerged a

A NEW ERA

range of retro models aimed specifically at attracting both old and young buyers and intended to recapture something of the glory days and romance of a bygone era. One of these, the Mojito, was unveiled in 2004 by Aprilia, another Italian company established immediately after World War II. Initially Aprilia built lightweight 50cc motorcycles and mopeds but over the next sixty years, the company earned huge respect for their endeavours in road-racing and trials competition. In 2010 they became the most successful ever motorcycle sports manufacture surpassing MV Agusta with an astonishing 276th victory. Nevertheless, it was not until 1990 that the Aprilia name was applied to a scooter. This was the Amico, the first scooter not only to feature plastic for its major non-mechanical components but a catalytic converter as well. The Amico was followed three years later by the Scarabeo, a four-stroke model with large diameter wheels and throughout the 1990s, a steady stream of models were launched alongside Aprilia's motorcycle range. In 2004, Roberto Colaninno's Piaggio & Co., S.p.A. bought out Aprilia along with its subsidiaries of Moto-Guzzi and Laverda. With these famous marques under Piaggio's overall control, it became the fourth largest motorcycle corporation in the World and could now compete on a more level footing with the likes of Honda and Yamaha. The company's export market was immediately expanded when the retro-styled PX range was launched in America shortly followed by a series of four-stroke engines introduced to comply with California's strict emissions legislation.

In 2010, a major milestone was passed in Tokyo when the Honda factory celebrated production the 60 millionth Honda Super Cub having been in continuous production since 1958. The C90 version remains the best selling scooter in the United Kingdom.

Also in 2010 and forty years after the manufacturing process had moved to India, the other name instrumental in helping to build an entire social movement was once again in production on Italian soil. Lambretta (now part of Lambretta Consortium) had returned home and although the task of final assembly was in the hands of a factory set up in Taiwan, the body panelling, styled on the chic scooters of the 1950s were being fabricated in Milan.

The Threes

THE THREES

Far Right: *In 2012, this Piaggio Ape was in use as an ice cream kiosk in Downtown Manhattan.*

In the late-1940s, Italy was struggling to recover in the aftermath of a crushing defeat at the hands of the Allied Forces during World War II, and with the road and rail infrastructure all but destroyed, the scooters of Innocenti and Piaggio amounted to one solution to the transport problem. This was okay for getting the general public mobile again but for local businesses that relied on collection and delivery of goods, the load carrying capacity of the two-wheeler was wholly inadequate.

With the Vespa already attracting much interest amongst potential purchasers, its designer, Corradino D'Ascanio was turning his attention to the commercial market and presented to company chairman, Enrico Piaggio, ideas for a three-wheeled version of his scooter. It basically represented a Vespa with the addition of a wooden flat bed at the rear over a pair of wheels on a common axle. Early in the development stages, it was quickly realised that the standard 49cc engine would prove underpowered for heavier loads and by the time the vehicle went on general sale in 1948, a 125cc unit was offered at extra cost. Initially it was given the model name TriVespa and then VespaCar (though this would later apply to a four-wheeler bubble-car built at the factory), until Ape (the Italian word for 'bee') was finally settled upon.

Three years after the Ape was first

unveiled, a 150cc version joined the catalogue with the wooden body replaced by a pressed steel bed. But it would not be until 1956 that the owner of a newly-purchased Ape could enjoy the luxury of an all-enclosed cab fitted as standard. At the same time, the engine was relocated to under the driver's seat, and although this meant that driving the Ape could often be a noisy and fairly hot experience, the Ape remained in this configuration for the next decade. In 1968 the position of the engine

was moved to the rear of the vehicle abating noise levels within the cab. Since 1948, there has never been a break in production and today the Ape is just as popular finding customers in developing countries and continues to be a rapid and cheap form of lightweight truck.

The Ape was by no means the first commercial vehicle to utilise the scooter concept as a starting point, however, and Abbotsford tried to capitalise on the idea as early as 1919. The Kingston-based firm looked as though it was trying to attract

itinerant vendors or at least get a foothold in the door-to-door delivery vehicle market with its rather optimistically named Supa Scooter. This strange little machine was powered by a 1.5bhp John four-stroke engine driving the two rear wheels via direct transmission. The riding position was something of a sit-up-and-beg affair with a crude tubular-framed stool-like seat equalled in level of sophistication by the most rudimentary flat wooden foot-board. At the rear was provision for carrying goods with

a choice of rack or lockable box. This was located directly over the back axle and without the operator sat astride the machine to counter-balance the weight, any ill-judged load distribution would almost certainly have resulted in the Supa Scooter upending. In a matter of months, the Motorpony (as it was also known) had understandably disappeared into the annals of history.

In France P. Poinard, who up until World War II had been a sidecar coachbuilder, decided to diversify in

the late-1940s and created a series of three-wheeled runabouts for both private and commercial use. In terms of styling, these were quite unremarkable and like the Motorpony failed to sell in significant numbers.

The German company, Hans Glas GmbH, had originally been established in 1883 to make agricultural implements and it was not until after World War II that Andreas Glas decided to try his hand in the motor vehicle industry. Between 1951 and 1969, Glas built a range of vehicles that in the early years included the Goggo scooter, followed later by the Goggomobil saloon car and commercial van. Before going into mass production, the Goggo was extensively tested and

given a seal of approval by the well-known ex-road racer, Georg Meier, winner of the 1939 Isle of Man Senior TT. Goggos sold well in Britain with the sole concessionaires being Lloyd Doig & Co. Ltd, London.

In December 1953, the Glas works at Dingolfing commenced production of a 3-wheeled utility vehicle based on Goggo mechanicals and in total, 485 examples were completed. Several years later, Glas were bought out by BMW for DM91 million and the Bavarian factory was subsequently expanded to cope with large scale car manufacture including the 3, 5 and 7 Series BMWs.

Another German firm, Fahrzeug und Maschinenbau Gustav Kroboth, unveiled

the Allwetterroller ('all-weather scooter') in 1955. As its name suggests, this two-seater microcar with its occupants seated side-by-side could provide good protection against wind and rain not only from the folding roof, but also because it was fitted with a full-width windscreen – a readily available component originally made for the Beetle by Volkswagen. The Allwetterroller had a central tube chassis, transverse leaf springs at the front, longitudinal at the back and was powered by a Fichtel & Sachs engine. After briefly dipping his toe in the world of motor manufacture, Gustav Kroboth decided enough was enough and in a complete change of direction, he embarked on a career as a driving instructor!

Switzerland has never been famed for its motoring heritage and there have only been a handful of firms specialising in scooters to bolster the country's industrial standings amongst its European neighbours. Indeed when respected engine manufacturer, Condor, decided to try their hand in the scooter market, they looked across the border into Austria for inspiration. In 1953, they secured a licence with Puchwerke AG, part of the Steyr-Daimler-Puch organisation, and began constructing a Condor-branded

Above: *The narrow track of the Ariel 3 is clearly demonstrated in this image. Note the rider beginning to lean into the corner whilst the rear engine pod remains level with the road.*

Above: *To add to the carrying capacity of the diminutive scooter, some companies provided sidecars as an optional extra. This example was manufactured by Squire of Bidford-on-Avon, Warwickshire.*

Ariel had during the 1930s, '40s, and '50s earned an enviable reputation as manufacturers of top quality British motorcycles. Nevertheless, by the mid-1960s, the two companies had merged and with competition from the mighty Japanese corporations effectively putting an end to the world-dominating British bike, other markets had to be considered. It was hoped the solution would come in the form of the Ariel 3, a three-wheeler quite unlike anything seen before. The age old problem with rigid tricycles was that they could not lean into corners. With the Ariel, this was overcome by a 'Tri-Torque' pivot between the moped-style front and the engine pod at the rear that contained a single-cylinder 49cc 1.7bhp Anker-Laura engine, a centrifugal automatic clutch and belt drive to one of the two narrow track rear wheels. The idea was patented several years before by G.L. Wallis & Son, an engineering firm hailing from Surbiton. Whilst the back end stayed level to the road, the rest of the bike could be ridden like a conventional scooter thus giving greater handling qualities and, when not in use, a self righting system kept the machine upright. Wheels and body panels were of pressed steel and by fitting

version of the RL25 at their factory in Courfaivre. For reasons that are not quite clear, a three-wheeled version was added to the range which could only have hampered fuel consumption.

As the next decade dawned, it was the turn of the British and two names once held in high esteem the world over for quality and reliability. Going on pedigree alone, BSA's Ariel 3 had promised so much yet failed to deliver and in the end was a sales disaster. Both BSA and

the optional extra windscreen in addition to the standard plastic leg shields, the rider could benefit from adequate protection during inclement weather. Appropriately, the 3 was available in only three colours – Everglade Green, Pacific Blue or Bushfire Orange.

Unveiled to the public in 1970 during a period in British transport history dogged by fuel shortages, petroil consumption of the Ariel 3 was quoted at a commendable 125 miles per gallon,

but even this could do little to boost sales. With the writing on the wall for the ailing BSA Group, even the marketing team seemed resigned to their fate and struggled to find the right words for the 3's advertising campaign. In describing its attributes, they could only come up with the dismally lacklustre "…you'll find the dullest trip seems a little more fun".

It took another ten years before the Wallis patent articulating pod was used

LITTLE BOOK OF **SCOOTERS**

again, this time by the Honda Motor Company. Although the first model, the Honda Stream, was only in production for two years from 1981 to 1983, the giant Japanese corporation enjoyed more success and attracted better sales with the concept than BSA. The Stream differed from the Ariel 3 in that both wheels were driven off the continuously variable transmission and the body panels were plastic instead of pressed steel, but buyers were put off by its high price tag.

It also lacked sufficient cargo-carrying facilities which were addressed in the following incarnation, the Honda Joy. The next two versions, the Just and the Road Fox offered two-speed automatic transmission, the latter model departing away from the fully enclosed scooter with its engine exposed in the open tubular frame – an attempt perhaps to attract a younger market.

Whilst the Stream, Joy, Just and Road Fox were intended for private owner

Above: The Moto Piaggio three-wheeler or MP3, featured twin front wheels, lockable suspension and a parking brake.

of Honda's articulated three-wheeled models were powered by a 49cc two-stroke engine until 2008 when it was replaced by a suitable four-stroke unit. In that year, the UP was also discontinued. At the time of writing, the X and Canopy were still part of the Honda light commercial carrier range.

In the 1970s, Scooters India Limited (SIL) acquired from British Leyland all production rights to the Lambretta name and moved the entire factory infrastructure, lock, stock and barrel, from Milan to an industrialised area south-west of Lucknow. Alongside the scooter range, SIL introduced the Vijai Super series, vehicles aimed specifically at the commercial market and which included the Vikram three-wheeler. These proved the more profitable of the two lines and, in 1997, the decision was made to discontinue scooters altogether and concentrate all efforts on commercials. Today, the Vikram model is exported to every corner of the planet and has been built in all manner of guises from open truck and delivery van to ambulance and minibus. They are particularly popular in third world countries with a proportionate number having been exported to Bangladesh and the Sudan.

use, Honda decided there was a definite need for something similar catering for small-scale delivery services. A year after the Stream entered production, examples of a commercial carrier called the Gyro X started leaving the Tokyo factory. The X was the first of three Gyro variations and was furnished with racks on both the engine pod and ahead of the handlebars. The UP which was built from 1985 had an enlarged pick-up style body at the rear, and the heavier Canopy, included in the catalogue from 1990, was so called because of the addition of an open-sided cab as well as a lockable box body. All

In 2006, Piaggio decided to make a bold attempt on the three-wheeler market and unveiled the MP3. Unlike the other machines mentioned in this chapter, the two wheels on the MP3 were located at the front and when cornering both tilted with the bike through a unique and complicated suspension arrangement. When not in use, the suspension could be locked at the touch of a button preventing the scooter from falling over which meant there was little need for a bike stand (although one was fitted anyway in case of battery failure). Conventional scooters rely on the stand to stop them running away if parked on an incline, so a braking system had to be incorporated to automatically apply simultaneously with the suspension lock. Since it first went on public sale, five engine options were made available from 125cc up to 500cc. In 2009, the MP3 LT400 was launched. This differed from previous versions in that the front track was designed wide enough to alter classification of the vehicle from motorcycle to tricycle status thus allowing it to be driven with a standard car driving licence and without the need for helmet protection.

In that same year, a fleet of hybrid petrol-electric MP3s were delivered to the New York City Police Department and though the additional battery cells increased the overall weight and in turn affected maximum speed, it could nevertheless accelerate from a standing start to 60 miles per hour in just 5 seconds! Equally impressive was that initial trials returned typical fuel consumption figures of over 140 miles per gallon indicating the possibility of huge savings in the NYPD's operating budget.

Above: *In Europe, the 500cc version of the MP3 was also marketed as the sporty Gilera Fuoco 500ie.*

A Cult Following

Like all major pastimes, there have been numerous monthly publications that, over the years, have been dedicated to celebrating the important role the diminutive scooter has played as part of the world's motoring heritage.

Magazine titles such as Scoot!, Scooter & Three Wheeler, Twist and Go, Classic Scooterist Scene and Scootering, have always focussed primarily on the bikes themselves, with written articles documenting in detail restorations and customisations, as well as delving into the archives making rarely-seen photographic material and ephemera available to the readership.

New products are often loaned to editorial teams so that they can be thoroughly tested and reviewed by a dedicated band of scooter enthusiasts. Interviews are also undertaken with leading figures within the industry so that those with a keen interest are kept bang up-to-date with manufacturing developments.

As part and parcel of scooter society a large section will be devoted to the latest lines in branded memorabilia, collectibles and artwork. But unlike practically any other vehicle-lead interest, 'scootering' encompasses a much wider interest that includes lifestyle, fashion and a genre of music that many young adults embraced in the 1960s, during the late-'70s/early-'80s revival, and from the 'Britpop' era of the early 1990s. Particularly during the

Above: *A splash of August Bank Holiday colour on Ryde Esplanade.*

last period, bands such as Blur, Primal Scream, Stone Roses, Paul Weller and to some extent Oasis promoted new albums, tours and any accompanying merchandise by using artistry and graphics that invariably included some form of scooter element, and once again tapped into a lifestyle born out of a cultural rebellion amongst the youths of the 1960s 'modern community'.

A movie that certainly chronicles this lifestyle better than any other was the 1979 film, Quadrophenia. Intended as another rock opera, it was written six years earlier by The Who after their success with Tommy.

Above:
'Mod'ification! Horns, mirrors, headlights, wire wheels, and lots and lots of chrome!

Centre: *The Royal Air Force roundel has been an adopted emblem of Mod culture since the 1960s.*

The Who were one of a number of bands emerging from the rhythm and blues era that epitomised the type of music that would eventually become most popular among the Mod community. Often fuelled by a cocktail of drink, cigarettes and amphetamines, sharp-dressed youths would dance throughout the night to the sounds of The Rolling Stones, The Small Faces, The Kinks and The Yardbirds.

Whilst the original musical element never made it to the silver screen, Quadrophenia could boast an all-star cast, though at the time, some had yet to make a significant impact in the world of film or music. The extraordinary list of talent included Phil Davies, Michael Elphick, Ray Winstone, Timothy Spall, Leslie Ash, Phil Wingett (probably best known as Jim Carver in The Bill), Patrick Murray (Mickey Pearce in Only Fools and Horses), Gary Holton (Wayne from Auf Wiedersehen, Pet) and John Altman (Eastenders' nasty Nick Cotton!). Two artists who would later be elevated to the top of the pop charts

during the '80s rock music subgenre, New Wave, were Sting who plays arrogant gang leader, Ace Face, and an almost unrecognisable Toyah Wilcox who takes the part of Monkey.

Quadrophenia is set in mid-1960s London when the Mod subculture was at its peak, and follows the fortunes of Jimmy Cooper, a young man disillusioned by his parents, his dead-end job and the world around him and who only finds solace and the freedom he craves at all night dances and riding his scooter in the company of fellow Mods. The period depicted was historically beset with a number of infamous battles that erupted between the fashion-conscious clean-cut Mods and their arch-rivals, the greased-back-hair biker boys, more commonly known as Rockers. Jimmy, played at that time by another relatively unknown actor, Phil Daniels, rides with his mates to spend the bank holiday in Brighton and is inevitably embroiled in a clash between the two opposing factions. Arrested by the police, he appears before the magistrates and receives a

Above: The image on this engine cover depicts a scene from the film Quadrophenia starring Leslie Ash and Phil Daniels.

Far Left: *The subtle customisation of this Lambretta includes a bank of air horns beneath the frame.*

Centre: *Custom modifications often go further than a simple paint job. This Lambretta pays tribute to the Battle of Britain with many features styled on the aircraft of World War II...*

Left: *...including mock machine guns!*

fine before returning to the capital and the drudgery he has been so desperate to leave behind him. Things get worse when he quits work, is kicked out of the house when his mother discovers Jimmy's drugs hoard and, ultimately, when his beloved scooter is destroyed in a collision with a Post Office van. Paranoid, isolated and seemingly with nobody to turn to, Jimmy takes the train back to Brighton only to find his idol, Ace Face, works as a lowly bellboy bowing and scraping to the clientele entering and leaving The Grand Hotel.

The film ends when Jimmy steals Ace Face's immaculate scooter, chrome plated and embellished with a mass of extra lights and wing mirrors, and rides it to Beachy Head. With The Who's I've Had Enough playing as a backing track, the last shots show the machine falling to the rocks below.

Although the movie was never a major smash at the box office, it has since earned cult status representing a fair portrayal of the Mod scene during 1960s Britain.

The chic little scooter has, in time, found supporting roles in many other

Above: *The Jam were a band popular during the Mod Revival of the late-1970s and early-1980s. The music of the era is a favoured topic for the beautifully rendered artwork that often adorns scooter body panelling.*

Centre: *This machine is decorated with hand-painted artwork commemorating the fire services of days gone by.*

films, such as Rebel Without a Cause, Octopussy and The Commitments. Roman Holiday, a 1953 release starring Gregory Peck in the leading role of reporter Joe Bradley, thrust leading lady Audrey Hepburn into the limelight winning her an Academy Award, a BAFTA and a Golden Globe. The film also provided a surprising boost to scooter sales, especially in America, where a number of stars amongst the Hollywood glitterati became new owners.

Over fifty years later, the 2004 remake of Alfie depicted the main character played by Jude Law riding the streets of New York aboard his Vespa. Numerous early Vespas and Lambrettas were also featured in The Talented Mr Ripley, another of Law's films starring alongside Matt Damon, Gwyneth Paltrow, and Cate Blanchett. The location shots of Turin during that ultimate of gold bullion heists, The Italian Job, serve as a good reminder of the sheer number of Vespas and Lambrettas that were predominantly part of the 1960s scene together with the ubiquitous FIAT 500. In 2010, Graham Greene's 1938 picture

Left: *One of the best scooter artists in the business is Dave Dickinson of Bridlington. Hundreds of hours went into the creation of this Vespa, aptly entitled Pulp Fiction.*

Brighton Rock was remade but this time set in 1964. Local scooter club members were asked to attend three days of filming, again to recreate the violent confrontations once encountered between a minority of Mods and Rockers.

With the Mod Revival of the late-1970s came an invigorated passion for the scene. The next generation of enthusiasts had taken the little scooter to their heart and regional clubs up and down the country began to form so that like-minded people could meet and admire the handiwork of fellow owners and restorers. Most of these organisations only seemed to offer membership to open frame Vespas and Lambrettas, however, and to cater for owners of the many rarer makes and models, the Vintage Motor Scooter Club was formed in 1985 with subsequent meetings attracting an incredible array of strange and interesting machines.

Events held up and down the country not only represent social gatherings for like-minded scooter fans and aficionados, but allow attendees to dress in the type of clothing that in

A CULT FOLLOWING

Right: *A panoramic view showing a sea of scooters on the Esplanade at Ryde.*

Below: *Hundreds of Vespas and Lambrettas prepare to board the Red Funnel ferry at Southampton ahead of the August Bank Holiday International Scooter Rally in 2012.*

the 1960s, set Mods apart from other fashion groups.

Taking styling influences from France and Italy, the dapper Mod uniform was typically clean cut and tailored for a close fit. Expensive suits, v-neck pullovers or cardigans, button-collar shirts, thin ties, and pointed 'winklepicker' or chisel-toed shoes all went to create the effect. To protect their clothes from the worst weather, Mods took to wearing a military-type overcoat called a Parka and the Royal Air Force red, white and blue roundel became widely used as a Mod symbol appearing on coats, scooters, publications and other graphics.

Both boys and girls adopted short-cropped hairstyles that, for the men, were always brushed forward, never back, and sideburns were the ultimate no-no!

Women wore round skirts over a many-layered petticoat or dresses, preferably the shorter and tighter the better that deliberately went against the wishes of their conservative

parents who were generally regarded as 'square'! Narrow-leg trousers, often with a button or two at the ankle, flat shoes, false eyelashes and sexy pale lipstick emulated a look that was championed at the time by the likes of London designer, Mary Quant, and fashion model, Twiggy.

Today's national and regional events also serve as a platform for both up-and-coming and established bands. The music is largely a mixture of African American soul, Jamaican ska and sixties rhythms, and acts such as FuzzFace, The Hamsters and Moses, as well as the likes of Who's Who, The New Age Jam and The Small Fakers – groups that pay tribute to bands of the past – provide a steady program of nightly entertainment.

The most popular meeting venue for scooter owners is Ryde on the Isle of Wight where the International Rally held every August Bank Holiday tends to attract thousands of riders from all over the country, Europe and beyond.

Below: *A swarm of scooters about to head through the streets of Ryde towards Sandown.*

Lost in Translation

Whilst the vast majority of scooters produced came out of the Italian factories of Piaggio and Innocenti, these companies preferred to list their Vespas (meaning 'wasp') and Lambrettas (derived from River Lambro in Milan) using a consecutive numbering system.

Elsewhere, however, other brands and models either adopted appropriate titles to distinguish their role in a particular market sector, or were endowed with a baffling and bizarre array of identities that one can only wonder as to how they were come by.

Scooters were especially popular with women – the step-through configuration, for example, being more refined than having to swing one's leg over a motorbike saddle. Scooter companies realised there was a huge market amongst the female population and began promoting their products in a range of bright and attractive colour schemes designed specifically with feminine appeal. Accordingly, the models on offer were given names aimed at engaging with potential lady owners. In the 1960s, Triumph advertised the Tina and Tigress, both very much in the Lambretta/Vespa mould and in addition to the fairings, were available with a optional extra windscreen to protect the rider against inclement

Right: *A rather racy publicity shot for the 1961 Triumph Tigress.*

weather. In Cleckheaton, Yorkshire, Phelan & Moore (P&M) were promoting the Panther Princess whilst DMW who operated out of Wolverhampton were building the Bambi.

The German concern, Victoria, had obviously found its target audience when they launched such models as the Peggy and Nicky. These were colourful little machines, the latter being powered by the firms own design 50cc engine called the Vicky!

Back to Italy and the Piacenza-based Costruzioni Meccaniche Casalini not only manufactured mopeds and scooters but also very lightweight enclosed three-wheelers, providing a relatively cheap weatherproof alternative to their two-wheeled products. One of these was a 49cc microcar, a rather ugly contraption where the two tandem-seated occupants squeezed into a boxy steel body as wide as it was long, and surrounded on all sides by glass. To make matters worse, Casalini named this model the Sulky and anyone daft enough to buy one would almost certainly have looked a bit disgruntled when they realised

Right: *The Triumph Tigress was identical to the BSA Sunbeam (illustrated earlier) in all but name. Both were available with either 175cc two-stroke or 250cc four-stroke units.*

everyone else was laughing at them! It was also offered as the David, a four-wheeled version possessing an equal lack of interior space, or with an estate body called the Break, perhaps in anticipation of its eventual demise! It seems that Casalini liked the name 'David' so much that they used it for an altogether more pleasing vehicle, the B48 scooter first introduced in 1956. The B48's elegant streamlined bodywork completely enclosed all the workings but could be cleverly lifted, hinged at the steering headstock affording unobstructed access to the motor. Nevertheless, the thought

of admitting to your mates that you simply love to ride around town on your David probably meant it was not a great seller in this country.

190 miles to the south-east at Pesaro, it is equally doubtful whether Motobi were seriously considering the British export market either when

they first unveiled their Pic-Nic. Likewise the Viennese-made Lohner Sissy could only have struggled to attract orders among burly men of the United Kingdom but seemed to be a hit amongst the Austrian buying public and remained in continuous production for over five years. In the

late-1950s, the Dutch were riding Burgers! They had remaining loyal to Eerste Nederlandsche Rijwielfabriek, the first bicycle makers in Holland, who were selling a model named after company founder Hendricus Burgers.

In Japan, commuters chose to ride to work aboard the Silver Pigeon, whilst many others looked to the splendidly named Rabbit Superflow! The Silver Pigeon was Mitsubishi's saviour at a time when Japan was still reeling in the aftermath of World War II. In the preceding six or so years, the factory had concentrated all efforts on building the highly manoeuvrable Zero combat fighter aircraft but with the defeat of the nation at the hands of the Allied Forces came restrictions on the production of military equipment. Between 1948 and 1965, thousands of Silver Pigeons left the Kobe works, gradually being improved over time with better mechanics and more powerful engines. Two years before the Silver Pigeon hit the high street, Tokyo rival, Fuji, unveiled the Rabbit Superflow and while Mitsubishi eventually turned their attention to automobile manufacturer, Fuji's two-wheelers would sustain another two

years before the business closed.

Hailing from London, the Dayton Cycle Company Ltd's chunky Albatross, or indeed the East German-built IWL Troll could never have filled potential buyers with much confidence and for the French the story was no different. Normally content to embrace the eccentric, they bucked the trend and refused to adopt the ideas of Établissements Delaplace whose 85cc steed only made a brief appearance at the 1952 Paris Show. Had it received more enthusiasm, then perhaps Parisians could have toured the city riding the Horsy with aplomb. The Horsy may even have become part and parcel of the city's cultural scene as the Vespa had in Rome, but alas...

Yet the prize for the most ridiculous name allotted to any scooter model must surely go to Demm, a short-lived exercise that saw the Milanese firm enter the scooter market in 1957. When a customer purchased Demm's beautifully sculptured 49cc model, he could ride off into the setting sun with the knowledge that he was now the proud owner of a brand new Dick Dick!

Far Left: This Troll, short for IourenRoller Ludwigsfelde or Ludwigsfelde touring scooter, was built in East Germany by IWL and is owned by James Starrett of Weymouth, Dorset.

ALSO AVAILABLE IN THE LITTLE BOOK SERIES

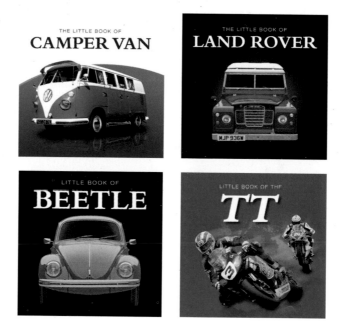